# An Apology
# to My Demons

The skeletons in her closet were not her enemies.
They were her army.

## Maiya Katherine

BLUE DRAGONFLY
LIFE

This edition published by Blue Dragonfly Life,
produced by Highpoint Executive Publishing.
For information, write to info@bluedragonflylife.com.

First Edition

ISBN: 978-1-7344497-1-6

Library of Congress Cataloging-in-Publication Data

Katherine, Maiya
*An Apology to My Demons*
*The skeletons in her closet were not her enemies. They were her army.*

Summary: "*An Apology to My Demons* is one young woman's story of how
an auto accident proved to be the catalyst for overcoming the self-destructive
habits and beliefs she developed over time to cope with trauma and abuse she
experienced in childhood and adolescence." – Provided by publisher.

ISBN: 978-1-7344497-1-6 (paperback)
1.Self-Help

Library of Congress Control Number: 2021914951

Cover and Interior Design by Sarah M. Clarehart

Manufactured in the United States of America

# Contents

# Dedication

For all whose heart was hurt by another
For all who were betrayed by someone they loved
For all whose innocence was taken away
without their consent
For all whose own mistakes still haunt them
to this day
For all who self-sabotaged without being aware
they were doing so
For all the misfits, the misunderstood, the weird,
the strange, the different, the unique
For the lovers of cherry blossoms,
pistachio ice cream, and sunflowers
For those who never fit in, those who do not want to
fit in, and those who will never fit in
For the invisible ones, the marginalized ones, the
overlooked ones, the so-called damaged ones
And for all my other Bear Cubs:

This is for you. All this is for you. Life is for you.
Peace and Love to you, always…

*Mama Bear*

**For Jedi Bear and Edgy Bear:**
One day I came to the line
The line between this world and the next
Standing between fighting and giving up, I looked
for a lifeline
A reason to persevere
And then I saw your faces
And I knew what I had to do
I had to fight
For you
For me
For Love
Everything I do is for you
I love you

**For the ones whose prayers have blessed me:**
Thank you (you know who you are).

**To my best friend:**
We felt each other's heartbeat, even before our eyes met
I am grateful to the Universe for creating you for me
And creating me for you
There are no words to fully express what you mean to me
So let me just say this:
It is you, it has always been you, it will always be you
I love you.

# Acknowledgments

To the ones whose pain, stories, and courage inspired me to heal my own heart, find my own light, and share it with others:

Louise Hay
Oprah Winfrey
Wayne Dyer
Lady Gaga
Kurt Cobain
Beyoncé
Tony Robbins
Sylvester Stallone
Abraham Hicks
Daddy Yankee
Bob Marley
Toni Morrison
Chadwick Boseman
Martin Luther King Jr.
Princess Diana
Will Smith
Maya Angelou, Maya Angelou, Maya Angelou
(and many more)
THANK YOU, THANK YOU, THANK YOU
(from my heart)!

# Prologue

She had finally mustered the courage
To open her Skeleton Closet, her Demon Closet.
She was ready to go to war
With the enemy who hid behind its doors, for years
. . . But all she found in there
Was an Army
Formed out of the relics
Of broken promises, pain, and despair
And that Army was ready to protect her heart
At all costs.
Even at the cost of her own emotional healing
Even at the cost of her long-term well-being...

# Rock Bottom

*"It is by going into the abyss that we recover the treasures of life. Where you stumble, there lies your treasure."* —Joseph Campbell

There is darkness inside her. She knows it. She tries to ignore it most of the time, but when something triggers her, the monster comes out. In a matter of seconds, a violent rage builds up inside her and starts spreading to her entire body, her mind, and her heart. The darkness usually creeps up slowly, but it is powerful and intense. By the time she realizes it has taken over her, it's usually too late. Tonight, as much as she tried to control her anger, the monster got the upper hand, once again. The look from the people in the room, the broken glass on the floor, the immediate headache she got from the rush of blood to her head—all lead her to realize that the worst happened: she blew up and blew up badly. She lost her shit, so to speak, and went off the rails, yet another time.

As she tried to regain her cool, she could feel the sting from all the disapproving stares of those looking back at her. She could sense the fear, disgust, and disappointment emanating from the people who had just witnessed her emotional breakdown. As with similar incidents before this one, she quickly went into justification mode and all the reasons why her reaction was justified, and why a certain word from another individual had caused her outburst. Like all the other times, someone else was to blame for her crazy behavior, or something had pushed her to react this way.

However, as hard as she tried to portray herself as the victim, deep down she knows the reasons why she exploded a little while ago. It was her demons' fault again. Yes, tonight, was one of those nights when her negative emotions and impulses, a.k.a. her demons, got the best of her and exposed her for who she really is: an emotionally broken girl, who is increasingly losing her ability to suppress the fury that had been festering inside her since childhood. Tonight, no matter how hard she had tried, she had lost control of the monster that she had been so desperately trying to hide for years.

She left the situation just like she departed all the other ones: kicking herself for not being able to get a handle on her feelings. As she took the shameful drive back home, she replayed the incident in her mind, wishing she would have reacted differently and hoping she could somehow go back in time and get a do-over. If she had another shot at this night, she would have used her wit, her sarcasm, and her ability to cleverly put people in their place, to retaliate against the girl who had made that smart-ass comment about her at the party. She would have gotten her point across and defended herself calmly, without looking like a lunatic. However, tonight, like all the other bad nights before, she would not have that second chance.

*You don't get a do-over, sweetie. Nope.* She was out of luck when it came to being able to fix the messes she created. She did not have a second shot last week either, when she blew up at work. At least at that time there wasn't a crowd watching her ugly metamorphosis. There was only one coworker who saw her losing control. But what about the week before that, when the corner store owner also witnessed her monster taking over? Why didn't he just have another bottle of the vodka she liked? Didn't he know how much she needed it?

It had been a tough week for her, a series of bad days that had forced her to deal with triggers from many of her childhood traumas. She had heard the news of a young actor committing suicide, and that had brought her back to some of her darkest days. She needed the alcohol to cope with the bad memories and bad feelings, and that particular brand of vodka was one that didn't bother her stomach too much. All she did was ask the guy at the counter to double-check if he had her favorite beverage in the back. So what if she asked a few times too many? She just wanted him to check, that's all. Why did he have to be so mean to her and ask her to leave, like a criminal? No wonder her monster came out. He asked for it, right?

Her recent outbursts were starting to stress her out, though. They were becoming too frequent for comfort. The vodka was not helping as much as it did before. Neither was the binge eating and purging. Nor was making out with more guys than usual. That was not doing the trick either, as it did in the past. Even the white substance did not give her the high it used to. She felt she was losing control of her mind. Her body was starting to revolt as well, and her stomach was getting increasingly sensitive to the things she ate and drank. Years and years of poor nutrition and toxic eating habits had taken a toll on her body. Everywhere she went now, she had to make sure she had access to a bathroom. And the bad memories…They, too, were relentless. Everywhere she looked, she swore she saw people who reminded her of Him. She could not think of Him. Of what he did to her. She did not want to think of it. *Oh God, please make me forget. I can't deal with it. I can't d…*

The last thing she remembered was a metal guardrail and cold water…

# The Invisible Scars...

*"Be kind, for everyone you meet is fighting a hard battle."* —Plato

She was in the water...in the car. Trapped. Thinking about some of her past emotional traumas had caused her to stop paying attention to the road, and her car had struck a metal guardrail that separated the street from the lake on the other side, a lake she used to admire during her drives to her apartment complex. The car was slowly sliding into the water, and she knew that things would only be getting worse and worse for her as time went by.

Stuck between this world and the next, she started thinking about her life. Was she experiencing what people said happened before you die? Was she seeing her life "flashing before her eyes"? Well, she was not really having flashbacks of her entire life. No. For some reason, all she could think about were the monsters hiding inside her — her demons, her fears, and the many skeletons in her closet that she felt were ruining her life.

*They caused my accident tonight,* she thought. *Fuck you, demons! Fuck you, skeletons! Look where you got me! Are you happy now? You are the reason why I may die today. I wanted my exit to be on MY terms. I did not want it to be this way. Shit! I still wasn't even sure if I wanted to go yet. Fuck you, demons! Fuck all of you! There are so many of you, ruling my life, driving me into chaos and turmoil...I did not even get a chance to expose you all. To expose Him for what he did to me. To tell the world about the terrible memories that were driving me to madness. To tell those who know me about how I was bullied as a child and how that messed me up, to this day! And now, if I die, people will blame me, and not you demon fuckers, for my fall from grace. No one will know that you guys were the ones driving me insane right into the abyss, right into self-destruction, this whole time...*

She was right. Very few people knew that she had gone through tough times in her life, and no one was aware of the extent of the emotional traumas she endured. Everyone hides parts of themselves in one way or another. In her case, however, she hid most everything about who she really was and what her past was like. Most people who came across her saw what she wanted them to see: a generally productive, self-reliant individual, who seemed in control of her life and future. What no one knew what that she was, in fact, someone constantly jumping through hoops and creating diversions so that she did not have to reveal the real her: a wounded animal, walking through life pretending she was okay.

She was a wounded animal, and she was not okay. She knew that. At the very least, she understood that something was broken in her, emotionally speaking. Over the years, the many unhealed emotional scars that she carried inside had created a lot of negativity in her life, including exaggerated fears, unhealthy eating behaviors, emotional triggers, low self-esteem, codependency, and other negative coping mechanisms. No one could see these, but she knew they were there, for they hurt every time a situation reminded her of the pain that caused them. She called those scars her demons, and she hated what they did to her. They made her easily triggered; they got her involved in toxic relationships; they made her cut her arms; they made her hate her body and do many other horrible things to herself and to others. She blamed most, if not all, of the problems in her life on those demons and was convinced that they were just out to destroy her.

Her demons were certainly pushing her into situations that

were not in her best interest and that got her heart and body broken time and time again. It was obvious in every aspect of her existence, including her personal life. For example, she constantly dated men who did not have their shit together, and she always ended up in relationships where she had to take care of a boyfriend financially. No matter how hard she had tried to meet stable guys, she seemed to only be attracted to the ones who had no real goals for their lives. It was one of her toxic relationship patterns, and she did not know how to break it.

She was convinced that she was this way because of what Mr. Peter did to her when she was a teenager. It was one of the worst things a person could ever experience, and many of her emotional scars had to do with what he put her through. Because he was powerful and influential, she felt almost sick when she had to deal with men who reminded her of Him. For this reason, she hung around guys who did not have anything in common with Mr. Peter. In other words, she only hung around men who could not pull their own weight. In her mind, all powerful men were just like Mr. Peter; therefore, all powerful men were bad.

*You see what you've done to me, demons,* she thought. *Now, I am about to drown here. I fucking hate you all.* Although the demons created by Mr. Peter's actions were the worst, they were not the only ones driving her into self-destruction. There were many other bad memories, skeletons, and demons taking residence in her being, influencing her actions: the memory of her so-called friend tricking her into being stuck in that car freshman year; the memory of feeling guilty because she stayed silent after witnessing men in her family betraying their marriages in plain sight; the memory of being essentially abandoned as a child by her caretakers while they partied nonstop with their friends; the memory of the schoolteacher telling her she was not beautiful enough to play the queen, and that she should, instead, play the servant; the memory of the lady at the beauty salon who always said that it was a good thing she was smart because she was not pretty

7

(similar comments were said in front of her family multiple times, but no one had ever defended her); and the memory of her best friend betraying her trust by blurting out a secret she had promised to keep private, just to mention a few.

The guilt and shame of having betrayed others was weighing heavy on her heart too. Those old wounds never left her, you see. They never stopped hurting. They just wove themselves into the fabric of her being. She hated them, and thus she hated herself, as they had become one with her. *Can you all just fuck off? Go away! Leave me alone! It's ten, twenty years later, already…Why can't you just LEAVE ME THE FUCK ALONE!!!?????*

But they lingered, those pesky little wounds. Still, no matter how they still hurt, cleaning out her demon closet for much needed emotional healing was not something she considered doing at all. No, a fight against her inner demons would be one she could not win, she thought. There were just too many painful memories for her to deal with. Too many scars for her to heal by herself. Her demons were too strong and too numerous, and all they wanted was to make her life a living hell. They were her enemies. Unlike most people who may have one or two catastrophic things happen to them in their lives, in her case, there was not just "a" skeleton in "a" closet, but rooms and rooms of abandoned cemeteries, filled with decaying bodies and bones. A repository of dead dreams, dead hopes, broken promises, betrayals, lies, and worse, violations of body, violations of trust, and violations of innocence.

Every inch of her reeked of painful experiences, silently festering and simmering below the surface, but she felt powerless against them. Despite the image of inner strength and poise she generally projected to the world, she did not feel strong on the inside. And lately, that image had become gradually harder to maintain as she felt increasingly powerless against the demons she had tried to suppress for years. Indeed, she was too afraid to even look at the emotional scars laid all over her heart. Even though she had survived many hardships, she saw herself as emotionally fragile, as someone who could not handle the toll of trying to heal the hurts her heart had suffered throughout her life. She had concluded at one point that even acknowledging the bad things that had happened to her would be something that could break her. She could not stand the thought of "going there," of looking back at the brutal experiences that had scarred her to her core. *It would be too difficult,* she thought, *to think about the stuff that had caused me so much pain, let alone to try to heal it.*

*Do you see us? Hey! Yes, you. Do you hear us?* When her old emotional wounds called out to her, she felt that her job was to shut them up, to smother them. She hoped that they would go away, eventually, as she put her attention on building what she thought was the perfect version of herself. The fake version. The proper one. The acceptable one. The one that fit the ideal life she thought she wanted to have.

Indeed, the main goal of her life was to become the very opposite of who she felt she was on the inside. She had to be anyone but herself because deep down, she knew that the real her was not good enough. In fact, she knew that the real her was not good, period.

# And the Oscar Goes to...Me

*"Never underestimate the pain of a person, because in all honesty, everyone is struggling. Some people are just better at hiding it than others."* —Will Smith

The coldness of the water around her feet brought her back to the present. She immediately noticed that only the front of the car was currently submerged. Nevertheless, the situation was dangerous as she could feel the water slowly rising in the vehicle. As she contemplated her next move to try to get out of the car, she thought about the many times she had close calls, emotionally speaking, when she felt she was going to lose her mind and succumb to the inner turmoil that had plagued her for many years of her life. Yet, she had always managed (well, until recently) to appear as if she was in control of her feelings and was emotionally stable. Yes, pretending she was okay was something she used to be good at.

She should have been an actress, she used to think. In a way she was. Portraying herself as someone she was not had been her mission for years and had been pretty easy for her most of the time. It was all about just playing a part. *Lights, camera — drugs, alcohol, and lies — action!* Making herself look well-adjusted was of the utmost importance to her, as she knew the real her would never be accepted, let alone admired by the society around her. She was messed up, she was damaged goods...and no one wanted to be around damaged goods.

For many years things generally went according to plan. If you asked her coworkers, hairstylist, or cousins to describe her, there would mainly be words of praise, admiration, and even gratitude. Even those who sometimes clashed with her would tell you that they respected her determination, her work ethic, and her no-nonsense attitude. From the time she had started high school, all she did was accumulate accomplishments: top student, class representative, three-season athlete, college scholarship recipient, and so on. After high school, not even the sky was the limit. People who knew her would say she was a rising star. Perfect job, perfect apartment, multiple awards for various things…She was the image of success. She had it all. She had to have it all. Anything and everything to distract the world and herself from who she knew she was inside: a wounded, broken, low-esteemed, ugly, stupid, fat, shy little girl, who hated herself, hated her past, and felt that life had let her down.

*If a psychologist ever got into my head, he or she would recommend me for depression treatment, therapy, or confinement,* she often thought, the last being an option that sometimes did not look so bad, considering she already felt stuck in the prison of her made-up persona.

Although she talked highly of herself when she was with others, she put herself down constantly when she was alone. You see, inside this head of hers were constant rage and self-defeating messages.

Years of hiding who she really was had caused her to loathe herself. She saw herself as a fraud. She was a fraud. Although she was fooling the world on the outside, on the inside, she engaged in self-criticism every chance she got. Her never-ending negative self-talk eventually turned her self-image and self-esteem to garbage. She did not like herself and she convinced herself that she was not a good person. She overreacted, she was sneaky, she put herself in bad situations, she lied, she was just a horrible human being, and she had started to believe she deserved the horrible life she was living. The hate she felt for those who hurt her in the past was slowly, but surely, starting to be directed at herself. *She* was the bad person now.

And because of that, she deserved all the bad things happening to her. The past emotional wounds were one thing, but the new ones she seemed to keep attracting to herself too easily and too often seemed like they were wounds she asked for, like being thrown out of the convenience store that day. It was her karma. As a result, she had resigned herself to a life of pain and hardship. A long time ago, an uncle had told her that people born under the astrological sign of Aquarius were doomed to suffer in life. Maybe he had been right. Maybe suffering was her destiny.

And so she suffered, and suffered, mostly in silence. *I am a survivor*, she secretly thought, *and surviving is now my life mission.* It was her story, and she took on that title of survivor with misguided pride. Every struggle she was able to overcome silently she saw as a small win against her demons. Not once in her wounded heart and mind did she understand that identifying solely as a perpetual victim could mean not only accepting a life of suffering, but also *expecting* a life of suffering.

She did not understand that this mindset would lead her to not discern, up front, that some situations were not going to be good for her well-being. She did not know that this mindset would push her into the arms of people who did not have her best interest at heart, for they themselves did not value a life based on compassion, love, healing, and honesty. She did not understand that this mindset would make her suspicious of good relationships and good people, for her subconscious fears felt validated when she encountered toxic situations.

Suffering was what she was used to, and unbeknownst to her, she sought situations that mirrored the emotional wounds she had not healed. In love, she kept following patterns that always ended with her having a broken heart. It would be years and years before she would one day understand that her fears and unwarranted mistrust were so intense that they were blocking her from fully opening herself to receiving real, true love. Not the kind of love story she saw in fairy tales she read as a child, but rather the kind of love that was nurturing, supportive, and respectful — one that would inspire her to become the best version of herself and reach her highest potential.

There were just too many scars left on her heart for her to have any chance to reach that high potential, she thought. At no point did she feel that true love and happiness were things she deserved or would ever enjoy. She was too damaged for that, too broken inside to attract anything other than grief and sorrow. She needed to act the part of a stable girl. She needed to hide her demons and her fears.

However, lately she was slipping. This year, she would not get the Oscar for Best Actress, she thought. After the incident tonight, or the one at the liquor store, or the one at work last week, her cover was starting to be blown. People were starting to see through her acting. She was slowly losing her ability to fake it. She was going to fail, she thought. *I cannot even succeed at being fake! That is how worthless I am. That is how broken I am.*

Unbeknownst to her, somewhere deep down inside, her heart was on a mission to destroy her pretend "acting career" before her pretend acting career destroyed her...

# The Stubborn Heart

*"Where there's hope, there's life. It fills us with fresh courage and makes us strong again."* —Anne Frank

As the cold water continued to rise above her ankles, she came out of her deep thoughts and started to look for ways to get out of the car. *I hope that at least one of the neighborhood's residents had heard the sound of my crash and has called an ambulance or the police,* she thought to herself. Although she did not feel she had broken any bones, she was starting to feel some pain slowly creeping up on her. *I need to get out of this car,* she frantically thought. *I probably will be taken to the nearby hospital.* She knew exactly where it was, for she had been admitted there many times. She remembered the time it was a very close call.

"If you did not come to the hospital, you would have most likely died tonight."

Those were the words of the doctor who treated her after her accidental overdose a few years prior. That fateful day, a long time ago, she missed death by a thread. It had started as a regular day, rather uneventful, but ended with her frantically making an emergency call around 11 p.m., as she felt this time, she could not fix herself alone. It was one of those nights when her demons came out to play — a night when she could not escape the bad memories that sent her to a dark place. She had taken more pills than usual, hoping that a stronger dose would finally allow her to sleep. However, as she started drifting into what could have been her final rest, she got scared and called 911. *What if I've taken too much?* she thought. *What if it is fatal this time?* As much as she had contemplated dying as a welcome relief from the turmoil inside, she had never gotten to the point where she had actually looked at death as a serious option. Maybe she was not strong enough to take such a drastic measure? Maybe she was too scared to do it?

Or was it that somewhere, deep inside, she did not really want to die? Was there maybe some hope that things could change for her?

There *was* hope. There is always hope. There had always been hope, on the inside, in spite of her not acknowledging it. As much as she had tried not to focus on them, sometimes old but pleasant memories made their way to her mind — memories of the times in her life when she was happy.

It seemed like it was lifetimes ago, but during some periods of her life, she did experience happiness for a little while. She did not want to think of those times, as they did not fit with the narrative she had created for the remainder of her life. She was broken and would never truly be at peace again or happy again. *So, why think about good times that will never come back?* she used to ask herself.

However, occasionally, when her demons took a break from harassing her, she would put her hand on her heart for a brief second and wonder what it would be like to feel joy again. To feel at peace again.

That is what she was missing the most: peace. What would it feel like to finally be free from her demons? As it turns out, although she had not yet realized it, her mind was not the only one dreaming of peace...

Her heart was dreaming also, as it, too, remembered happier times years ago. It was a heart that beat for her nonstop, even as she had slept, even as she had cried, even as she was unable to find any more tears to cry. That heart had never stopped dreaming of better days. This heart of hers had never agreed to living a miserable life.

That is why it still beat, even as she wanted to die, even after being violated, even as she stuffed herself with toxic substances, even as she forced herself to throw up every night, even as she drank herself to sleep, too often.

The same love and energy force that allowed her to survive her hardships and got her to build a life of apparent success despite her troubles had never accepted a life of pain for her. While she focused all her attention on the hardships she had experienced in her life, she had failed to acknowledge the one thing that kept her alive, the one thing that kept fighting for her even as she stopped fighting for herself.

She had failed to acknowledge the unconditional love her heart had always had for her. Indeed, it beat when she fucked up, it beat when she did good, it beat when she was high, and it beat when she was sad. It never judged her or asked her to meet certain criteria in order for it to keep beating. It just continued working, sometimes in treacherous health conditions she had caused herself.

Engulfed in self-criticism and hate for the ones who had damaged her, she did not give any consideration to the fact that she was still alive. Instead of focusing on the resilience that got her to survive all her hardships, she only focused on the hardships themselves and on the perpetrators.

As with many who are trapped in the images and feelings of bad memories, she had failed to understand that she needed to look at the other side of the coin, too, and not only focus on the bad memories.

*Yes, you went through all of that, but you are still here. Right, little girl? What does that tell you? It tells you that something, somewhere inside you, or something you think is outside your being is pulling for you, is fighting for you, is loving you, is on your side.* Although she could not see that from her wounded viewpoint, deep inside, her heart understood that she was a tiger. She was a warrior.

Her heart never stopped whispering hopes of a happy, better life. She did not hear those whispers often, but they were as relentless as the painful memories that kept crying out to her time and time again. For a long time, her heart's pleadings were too weak to compete against the loud screams of her demons, but they were there, nonetheless. It was like something inside her could not give up on life and didn't want her to, either.

Was that the reason why she could never pull the trigger — why she could never finish the bottle of pills? Was that the reason why she could never jump off the Golden Gate Bridge? She did not know. All she knew was that she had gotten to the edge many times, but she had never been able to end things. Lord knows how much she wished she could have. She just wanted to end the inner conflict, end the pain, end the unhealthy eating habits, end the sorrow, end the self-loathing. She just wanted peace. She just wanted peace, God…

# The Hammer and the Bullies…

*"Don't you worry your pretty little mind. People throw rocks at things that shine."* —Taylor Swift

Cold water on parts of her body snapped her out of her dream-like state. *Did I pass out again?* She could not tell how long she had been in the lake, but she knew she needed to get out of the car before it filled up with water.

*Why am I feeling such cold air?* she asked herself.

*Oh! The window was halfway open, stupid! You were smoking, remember?*

Smoking had been one of those habits that kept her anxiety down, and unlike the other illegal substances she used to cope with her inner chaos, fortunately it was one she could have in broad daylight. *Thank God! Something I can do without having to hide it for once…*

She had picked up the habit in high school, right after developing debilitating feelings of anxiety in middle school. While a breakup with a boyfriend was the worst thing that had happened to most of her classmates by the ninth grade, she had already gone through much worse by that time.

Unlike some of her peers, a broken nail was not the end of the world for her. She knew what the end of the world really meant, for hers had been crushed and destroyed many times before her freshman year. By the time she was fourteen, she had gone through things most people would never experience in a lifetime. She had gone through things that drove some kids she knew to addictions, which ultimately sent them to their graves. She had heard that some adults who had experienced the violations she had dealt with could not heal from them even twenty or thirty years later! Some of these adults had ultimately taken their own lives too, having succumbed to the pressures of their own demons. *Would that be my fate too?* she thought. *Why did so many bad things have to happen to me? Why am I stuck in a car again, like in high school, not able to get out?*

Again? Oh, yeah! It was not her first time being stuck in a car, but the last time at least death did not seem as imminent as it did tonight. *Why did those bullies from my old high school lock me up in that car that day?* The shame and hurt of that incident many years ago were still with her, and some of the demons causing her recent outbursts were related to that awful day during her freshman year. The bullying was so bad that she kept missing school days until she was almost expelled. Being shoved in the hallway and being cyber-bullied on social media were one thing, but being locked in a car that horrible spring day was by far one of the most frightful and humiliating things those bullies did to her. The worst thing was that no one seemed to have missed her that day. No one came to her rescue. As they stood there, laughing at her helplessness, her bullies did not understand that years later, that afternoon would be one she still had nightmares about.

It would become one of those memories that to deal with she needed her favorite vodka. It was one of those memories that she purged for. It would be one of those memories that caused her to not trust people easily — to always be skeptical of those who wanted to help her for no apparent reason, for that was how those bullies got her that day.

That is how her supposed friend Melody tricked her that day, pretending to have hidden some pot in her brother's vehicle that they both could smoke. However, when she got in the car, Melody pushed the door and was soon joined by a group of other ninth graders. She immediately knew something was wrong. She was stuck inside; the car doors were jammed.

She could still see her bullies' faces light up as they laughed at her and made fun of her obvious fears. Did they plan to come back later to get her? She would never know the answer to that question. As the sun started setting and panic started to creep up on her, she understood she had to try to get out of the car somehow. She proceeded to look under every seat, pick up every rug, and finally she found an old hammer under the front passenger seat. With all the strength of her fourteen-year-old arms, she hit the driver's side window multiple times until it shattered enough for her to pass through.

A small cut on her left thigh was all the physical evidence that remained from her heroic escape. However, that incident had left huge emotional scars on her heart that were not visible to the outside world. It caused her nightmares and created fears and demons that showed up every time she got into someone else's car. The damage from that day was so great that she even carried a hammer in her own car, due to fears that she may be locked inside there one day...*Like tonight?*

*Holy shit! The hammer...I've got a hammer in the car...*

# Déjà Vu, All Over Again...

*"Turn your wounds into wisdom."* —Oprah Winfrey

They say that sometimes, when you are facing death, minutes feel like hours and hours feel like minutes. It was not clear to her how long she had been in the water, but it felt like an eternity.

The cold water was rising toward her waist. Fortunately, she realized that her car had fallen in the lake in such a way that water was slowly getting in, but not rushing. That meant she had time to work on getting out — time to look for that hammer. After struggling a bit with her seat belt, she was able to locate it. And just like that time in high school, she was doing this alone. No one was coming to her rescue. It was like déjà vu, all over again.

Didn't anyone hear her car break through the guardrail? Where was the ambulance? Was she always going to have to fend for herself? Was that her destiny, to always have to save herself, by herself? Well, if it was, tonight was not the night she was going to answer that question. The most pressing thing now was to get out of the lake and freezing water. So, just like in high school so many years ago, she hit the driver's side window with the hammer with all her might. Again and again. And just like the time before, she grabbed her bag and pulled herself out, but this time, she suffered way more than one laceration in the process.

As she began to climb back onto the main road, she could see the flashing lights of an approaching ambulance. A police car was right behind it. *Oh, great,* she thought. *Now you come? Now that I'm out of the car, all scratched up? Thanks a lot!*

Although she just wanted to go home, the paramedic told her that she needed to be taken to a nearby hospital for observation and possibly testing. Her cuts were obvious, and it was apparent that they needed to be tended to. *Maybe they also wanted to check my alcohol level?* Surprisingly, this was not going to be the night she got booked for a DUI. Nope. The argument at the party she had run away from had started just after she had taken a sip of her first drink, and she had left after throwing her wine glass at the wall. *No, officer. I am not even drunk tonight. I am sober, for once. I just crashed because my demons clouded my thinking and eventually my vision, and I stopped paying attention to the road. For once, I am not under the influence. Maybe under the influence of my demons, but not of alcohol. No, not tonight.*

Her official explanation was that she tried to avoid some animal on the road. Then came the question that would eventually turn her life upside down: "How did you get out of the car?" the officer asked.

# A Different Perspective

*"If you change the way you look at things, the things you look at will change."* —Wayne Dyer

Officer: "How did you get out of the car?"

Her: "I had a hammer."

Officer: "You just happened to carry a hammer in your car?"

Her: "Yes, officer."

Officer: "May I ask why?"

Her: "Because of the bullies."

Officer: "The bullies?"

Her: "Some bullies locked me in a car when I was in high school, but I was able to get out because I found a hammer under the front passenger seat. When I got my first car, I decided to always keep a hammer in my car in case I got stuck again."

Officer: "What? So, you expected to be locked in a car again?"

Her: "Well, hmmm, kinda, I guess…"

(As soon as she said it, she thought to herself, *Why do I feel bad saying that?*)

Officer: "Okay…It looks like tonight that bad experience in high school served you well."

Her: (silence)

Officer: "Are you okay?"

Her: (silence)

# Total Confusion

*"The wound is the place where the light enters you."* —Rumi

She did not utter a word after that statement from the officer. She could not. She just nodded and the paramedics asked her to get into the ambulance. Intense, contradicting emotions were taking over. All of a sudden, it felt like her world had been spun on its head. Her entire way of thinking about her bad experiences was put into question by one sentence from a police officer. With a few words, he had turned her mindset upside down and confused the hell out of her. *Did he really say that the bullying incident in high school served me tonight?* she asked herself.

As she lay in the back of the ambulance on her way to the hospital, she could not help but think about his statement. For years, the demons of that fateful afternoon in high school had created a lot of negativity in her life. She had never spoken to anyone about that day, until tonight. She had swept the memories of that awful situation under the rug, and they eventually joined the rest of the skeletons in her closet. That experience had traumatized her, had caused her sleepless nights, had made her suspicious of her friends, and had driven her to unhealthy thinking and unhealthy behaviors.

How could she reconcile these negative consequences with the officer's words? How could anything about that day be considered positive? It did not make sense, and yet, she could not deny the truth.

*Tonight, my fear of being stuck in a car again actually helped me survive the crash. I carried a hammer in my car because I was afraid, and that hammer got me out of the lake. Does that mean that my fears actually helped me tonight? Isn't fear a negative thing? I don't know what to think anymore,* she lamented. She was now at a complete loss, questioning her life view and her own thinking. *How can something that bad be turned into something good?*

Years later, she would be able to see things more clearly. Changing your perspective on painful experiences is not a matter of turning bad experiences into good ones. What hurt did hurt, and what was bad is still not okay. But you can change your perspective on past hurts and understand that doing so is not about the individuals who've hurt you. It's not about seeing them as good people suddenly. It's not even about the bad incidents themselves. *It is about you, your heart, your present, and your future.* It is about cutting the chains that bad painful experiences bind you with. It is about taking something from what happened to you in order to benefit yourself or others.

Can bad experiences teach you anything that you can use to better your life? Well, little girl, the answer is YES! It is always YES!

In her case though, it would be a long time before she not only understood that, but truly lived by it...

# The Beginning of the End

*"In order to rise from its own ashes, a phoenix first must burn."* —Octavia Butler

*God, where is my vodka? I don't want to be thinking of these things now. I just want to go home, pass out, and get back to my life.* She had been admitted to the nearby hospital and was told she would stay the night for observation.

Although the police officer's words had sparked something in her, she was still her old paranoid self, and her demons were working hard to make sure she did not entertain any thoughts that involve them. The events of tonight had shaken her up, but inside she still felt like the broken girl with old dysfunctional patterns that were always trying to pull her away from what felt unfamiliar. Right now, questioning the bullying incident of so long ago was a new thing for her, and any new way of thinking scared her and sent her into a panic.

As daunting as the confusion was, however, she could not get the officer's statement out of her head. She could not undo what had occurred a few hours ago during her brief exchange with him. Something in his words had hit a nerve, and she could not put the genie back in the bottle.

It puzzled her, and she wondered if what he said could also apply to the other bad things that had happened to her. If the officer were here, what would he say about the Mr. Peter incident? Or the Keera incident? Or when the lady at the beauty salon called her ugly and said it was a good thing she was smart…was there anything good about that? She wished she could find the policeman again and go through the list of all the emotional scars on her heart. Would he confirm that they, too, could be helpful, even lifesaving?

She did not know it then, but the questions she was asking herself that night were going to take her places she could not even dream of in her current state of mind. The search for the answers she was seeking was going to require her to jump headfirst into the unknown. And the answers were going to make her question everything she thought about life and about *herself*.

This process was going to mean retraining her mind to accept that her heart also needed to have a say in her behaviors and decisions. It was going to involve forgiving people for whom she had once wished death. Most important, it would mean forgiving herself. It was going to mean calling out her own bullshit, too, and taking responsibility for her behaviors. It was going to involve total transformation into something she could not yet conceive. She would have to be the caterpillar who did not know it was going to become a butterfly.

She would eventually have to lose everything she valued in order to gain everything she deserved.

It was not going to be easy. An inner chaos as formidable as the one that had been building up inside her for years would require an equally powerful action to fully dismantle it. It would take something radical and explosive to turn things around for her. Indeed, in order to stop the madness her life had become, the old her would first have to die.

She was scared of the questions she was asking herself, and even more afraid of the answers she may get. *Is this something I want to go into right now? Is this necessary?*

It was too late to turn back, though. She had to know. Ready or not, she was going to go there. To the demon closet. She had to put the officer's theory to the test and run his statement through all her bad experiences. She knew that meant she would have to jump, head-first, into the fire her demons had created to consume her. That was a scary prospect, but she needed to find out if there was anything about the other situations which damaged her emotionally that could also serve her, just like the bullying incident did tonight.

She did not know what she was going to do or how, but for some reason, even though her path forward was uncertain, she felt compelled to proceed. She was on a mission. "A mission from God," as the Blues Brothers would say. She would have to look at each of her demons one by one and put them to the test.

Something was happening to her, but she could not clearly articulate what it was yet. All she knew was that the officer's words had woken something up in her, and for once in her life, she had a feeling that it was not the monster inside her who was rising. She did not know it yet, but she was right. This time, it was a phoenix.

# Nobody Is Coming to Save You

*"No one saves us, but ourselves. No one can, and no one may. We ourselves must walk the path."* —Buddha

"Aren't you going to sleep?" It was a new nurse. It was a little after 11 p.m. and her old nurse had left for the day.

"I will try to sleep soon," she answered, although deep down, she knew it was going to be an all-nighter. She knew she had gotten to the point where there was no turning back. *I have to figure this out. I need to know if the officer's words are true, for everything,* she told herself, as she lay in the hospital bed.

For years, she had resisted looking into her emotional wounds. However, between her crash and the officer's words, something had shocked her emotional system, and she could feel that there was a chance that things would never be the same again for her. A part of her still felt worried about going in and facing her demons, but she felt it had to be done. She did not even want to hope for healing; she just needed to know if there was another way to look at what happened to her. She did not know how she would find the courage, wisdom, or know-how to go about opening old emotional wounds, but she had a feeling she would find a way. No matter how broken she had been, the fact that she had pulled herself out of the car showed her that she was still capable of doing some good things for herself.

No one had pulled her out of the lake. No. She had done it by herself, for herself. And that, alone, was a big deal to her.

A big deal it was, indeed. You see, at one point in her life, she had developed an overwhelming need to find something or someone to "save" her from her demons, to save her from fears, to save her from herself. One day she had bumped into a coworker who had praised the benefits of attending motivational seminars. Soon after, she had secretly started looking into them. Slowly but surely, they became an obsession, an insatiable need to hear something, anything, that would trigger a change in her mind and allow her to transform into an emotionally healthy individual.

Once she caught the self-help seminar bug, she was hooked, like a junkie addicted to drugs. And like many junkies, she did this in secret. She kept it to herself, enrolling in seminar after seminar, buying self-help CDs to listen to in her car, making vision boards, binge-watching motivational YouTube videos, and reading every self-help article or book she could find. Although she could understand the benefit of the wisdom of what she heard and read, any resulting emotional relief was, unfortunately, always temporary for her. Like an addict, she just kept wanting more, needing more, binging on one quick fix after another, trying to quench her thirst for positive life messages and satisfy her need for a lifeline, for any lifeline.

What she did not and could not grasp back then was that unless and until she cleaned up her inner chaos, no messages or wisdom she heard or read would or could ever fully stick and take root. Unless she activated her own internal wisdom and opened her heart to true self-love, she could not fully absorb the loving and healing messages the universe had been so desperately trying to get through to her for years, even through excellent motivational speakers.

One day, however, she would feel enormous gratitude toward the coworker who had helped her attend her first motivational seminar a few years back. She also would realize that although she may not have been ready, mentally, to fully embrace the lessons she heard there, her heart taken notes and used them to keep working on her under the surface. Like they say, "Never underestimate the power of planting a seed."

The hospital bed was comfortable, but her level of thinking was now so intense that she needed to be seated, to hold her head high. The transformation occurring inside of her could not be achieved lying down. No. She needed to sit for this. To be upright, at least, with her shoulders straight. *It was game time.* Time for serious business. One part of her was still afraid, but she was not stopping.

She put her hand on her heart and remembered the time before, at the hospital, when it kept beating for her, even as her iron levels were at a life-threatening low. Her heart would get her through, she thought—well, she hoped so at least. She took a deep breath and pressed the emergency button to call the nurse on duty. She was ready. *Grandma,* she said to herself. *Please look down on me and help me get through this.*

# You Know What You Need to Do

*"Write hard and clear about what hurts."* —Ernest Hemingway

Nurse: "You called?"

Her: "Yes. Sorry. This is not a huge thing, but could you please give me pen and paper?"

Nurse: "Pen and paper"?

Her: "Yes, please."

Nurse: "Oh, okay…"

She knew what she had to do. She needed to write. Write it all down.

# Pen, Paper, Music, Art, and Nature

*"Art is the only way to run away without leaving home."*
—Twyla Tharp

Before her life completely got out of control and she could no longer feel happiness in her heart, there were a few things that gave her soul some joy: writing, music, art, and nature. However, writing and listening to music were what she enjoyed most while growing up.

During one of her rare family vacations with her Aunt Jessie when she was about eight, she found a turquoise diary in a local shop in a beach community her family loved to visit. The moment she saw it and felt its unusual fabric cover, she knew she had to have it. Her aunt had given her some cash to buy herself some knickknacks, and she knew this purchase was worth every penny she had in the pocket of her small flowered dress.

Although she started writing in her turquoise diary the day she bought it, it wasn't until a couple years later that it became the repository of her inner turmoil, the keeper of her teenage dreams, the only place where the many hardships she endured were acknowledged. She had created a unique way to form sentences so that people would have a hard time deciphering what she was saying if they ever got hold of her diary.

This turquoise diary was the only place she expressed her real truths...well, that *and* the Wattpad online storytelling account she had created under a username she now regretted using. Everything she wrote in those two outlets was a testament of what she had been through. However, if someone took the time to carefully read between the lines, he or she would find another aspect of her, a whole other world that only existed in her mind. Yes, hiding in plain sight were love stories and love letters to crushes that never knew she existed.

As intense as her inner darkness was, her heart was equally full of fiery passion, love, lust, dreams, hopes. In between words of sadness and despair were phrases and phrases describing a love she desperately wished she could give to another. No one knew it, but deep down, she was a hopeless romantic, craving not only to feel loved but also to give love. She was even willing to love a little bit more than she was loved back. She was okay to sacrifice for love, as sacrificing for her *was* an act of love — *the ultimate act of true love*. It was Juliet dying for Romeo; it was the princess trading her palace for a tent in the street so that she could be with her poor suitor. Because she had gotten so little from others in the past, she did not expect to get much going forward. Because of that, she thought it was okay to give more than she received. That over-giving mindset would eventually create an eager-to-please demon in her, who would make her constantly sacrifice her needs to benefit others. That attitude would plague her life and crush her spirit time and time again until she would one day realize, the hard way, that she deserved, at least, as much as she gave.

When she wasn't writing, music was her other refuge. She would have been dead without music. She probably could last a day or two without food, but without music, life would be unbearable, she thought. In childhood, she could never find anyone to relate to. There were a couple of people who came into her life who were able to catch a glimpse of the inner turmoil she was experiencing, and who tried to understand it and describe it. However, no one she knew was ever really able to put into words what she was feeling inside.

When it came to music, though, some songs she heard on the radio seemed to be birthed out of the womb of her despair, of her sadness, of her desperation, of her secret wishes. They were so on-point with what she was feeling that she wondered if somehow, those who sang them or those who wrote them, were going through the same emotional pain she was...

"I felt he'd found my letters and read each one out loud." This was a lyric from one of her favorite songs, "Killing Me Softly with His Song," the Fugees version. Although she did not know who originally wrote the tune, that one line pretty much summed up the story of her life.

Indeed, it seemed like certain songs were definitely about her life, like "Last Kiss" by Taylor Swift, "No One But You" by Queen, "When the Party's Over" by Billie Eilish, "Scared of Lonely" by Beyoncé, "Lovely" by Twenty One Pilots, "Til It Happens to You" by Lady Gaga, "Un-Break My Heart" by Toni Braxton, or "Redemption Song" by Bob Marley, and so many more...It seemed like some of the songwriters had secretly sneaked into her room, opened her turquoise diary, read all her words out loud, and turned them into songs. How do they do that? She wondered. *How had they been able to open the vault of my hidden emotions and laid them out so clearly for the world to hear and see?*

Whatever the answer to that was, tonight, there would be no music, though. All she could do was write. Where was this nurse, already?

# The Demon List

*"Until you make the unconscious conscious, it will direct your life and you will call it fate."* —Carl Jung

As she waited for the nurse to come back, she took deep breaths. *Breathe,* she told herself, *deep breaths.* Indeed, intentional, deep, measured breathing was one of the rare things that calmed and grounded her. She had learned about the healing power of breathing exercises through one of those YouTube videos she had watched while looking for answers to her multitude of emotional problems. *Deep breath, my girl.*

She knew what she had to do: write. Just as she did as a teenager, she would let her pen lay out all her heart was feeling. *Yes, little girl.* Write it all down. On a piece of paper, she would list all her bad experiences one by one, and by name. She would list every incident she remembered that had scarred her emotionally, then write the following:

- What happened? (The skeletons in the closet.)
- What demons, patterns, triggers did I create to cope with the emotional trauma?
- Why have I been afraid to deal with it directly?
- Do I need professional help to get the answers I seek, or can I do this alone?
- What can this teach me (or what has it taught me) that can make me stronger/wiser (or *has* made me stronger/wiser)?

She wondered if she would be able to look at bad experiences in a new light, as the officer did a few hours ago, when it came to the bullying incident in high school. One by one, her demons would have to be identified and addressed. It was a daunting task, as unfortunately, each fear corresponded to a painful incident, a skeleton in the closet, a ghost, a name, someone she once knew and had tried to forget for years.

However, it was too late to retreat now. She promised herself she would stop for a bit if the bad memories became too painful to handle. If they did become unbearable, she was not going to give up the fight, though. She had decided that if she could not do this alone, she would consider seeking the help of a therapist or other professional. However, no matter what, one thing was certain: She was going to go through this process, one way or another. That, she knew for sure.

*Deep breath, my girl…you got this!* When the nurse left after providing her with the pen and paper, she wrote down two words: Demon List. She paused and thought about what it was going to take from her to do this. It was going to take all she got. Would she have what it took? There was no way for her to know that. However, it was too late. She needed to know, and that was that.

She took a deep breath, looked up to the ceiling, and once again asked her maternal grandma for courage. Then, slowly, she wrote the words that would change her life forever…

# Demon #1 — The Violated Child

*Pick your battles, little girl…You don't always want to rock the boat, do you now?* Her grandpa had told her that as they walked through her childhood neighborhood on the way to church for Sunday service. Her Aunt Jessie and her husband whom she called Uncle Marc, were away for the weekend and had left her in the care of her maternal grandparents. When she was younger, no one ever told her exactly why her own parents were not raising her, and why Aunt Jessie and Uncle Marc had gotten the job of bringing her up. Someone mentioned that her parents were just not stable enough to take care of a child, but nothing was ever fully explained to her.

The week before that walk to church, she had experienced something bad, and she wanted to tell someone about it. However, as soon as she mentioned Mr. Peter's name, her grandpa uttered those words about picking your battles, and the conversation about it was effectively over.

Mr. Peter was still Uncle Marc's friend to this day. Nevertheless, she wrote his name under "Demon #1" on her list. Over the years, she had tried to hint to other family members that Mr. Peter was someone she did not like and someone she did not want to be around ever again. She had hoped that Aunt Jessie and Uncle Marc would take the bait and ask her about her reasons for her dislike of him, but they seemed to not want to know. Mr. Peter was wealthy and well connected. He owned a yacht, a beach house, and a log cabin in

Maine. He was the type of person who would let his friends enjoy his possessions. "Peter is such a great guy," Uncle Marc would say. "He is generous and kind and loving." *Yeah*, she thought, *too loving...*

Mr. Peter's connections with the community and the world were extraordinary. He had managed to be liked by many hundreds of people by being very generous with his money. The local non-profits loved him. The clergy loved him. The politicians drooled at the sound of his name. Every middle-aged woman in town, and some middle-aged men, had a crush on Mr. Peter. He was awesome, most people felt, and if you didn't think so, you were crazy and looked down upon. Indeed, throughout the years, some community residents had complained about a few things Mr. Peter had done, but their grievances were never given the time of the day. You don't attack someone like Mr. Peter, her grandpa used to tell her.

Like others in his social position, Mr. Peter bet on others defending him. People like him understood that one way to control others is to make them dependent on you. And once you have them under your influence, they go to bat for you and defend you, even when you are wrong. That is why her grandpa had told her about not rocking the boat. Standing up against Mr. Peter was not a war people won, her grandpa said. If you've got something to lose, don't fight him. Don't rock to boat...

*But,* she thought, *did Mr. Peter care when he rocked MY boat?* That fateful evening, when Aunt Jessie and Uncle Marc, who were charged with raising her, had once again dropped her off at Mr. Peter's niece's house for babysitting, and Mr. Peter had come into her room and started talking to her, did he care about the long-term damage he was about to cause to her self-esteem, to her self-worth, to her self-image? Did he care about the world he was about to topple over, her world, the world he was about to throw into chaos, the heart he was about to bruise for life, the arms he was about to condemn to a life of cutting, the loss of her innocence? Did he understand how the demon of the violated child created in her by his actions made her shy away from powerful men all her life? Indeed, because of him, she found herself only dating men who did not have their lives in order, men who did not seem powerful. Consequently, she always had to shoulder more than her fair share in her relationships and ended up taking care of many boyfriends financially.

*Did Mr. Peter care about rocking my boat?* Her grandpa's words had lingered in her head long after his death. She had never said a word about the incident with Mr. Peter to anyone due to fear of retaliation from her assailant, and due to the humiliation and shame that she carried as a result. She had tried, year after year, to forget that horrible evening, but the bad memories just kept haunting her. She had to endure that some of her family members were still friends with that monster, which meant she still had to see him at family functions and hear her Uncle Marc praise his name over and over.

Yes, Mr. Peter's action that night created demons and fears inside her and gave her nightmares that caused her many sleepless nights. It left her with triggers that brought her right back to that traumatizing incident. For example, every time she felt that a person was trying to push her to do something she did not want to, she immediately felt pressured, as she did that night, and thus, she reacted with way more force and anger than was required. It was the violated child demon deciding to show toughness first, right off the bat, in a subconscious effort to try to discourage her perceived "assailants" from trying to overpower her into doing something she did not want to do. Whenever that feeling came up, even in non-romantic relationships, it made her monster come out even when she could have addressed the situation with less aggression. She had never been successful in repressing this horrible episode of her life involving Mr. Peter, and lately it had gotten to the point where the drinking and purging and cutting no longer quieted the memories of that awful evening.

*Where was that police officer now — the one who turned my world upside down by casually commenting that my bad experience in high school served me well in escaping my sunken car? How could anyone find a silver lining in losing their innocence? How could anyone possibly find a positive in this horrible event?*

*Deep breaths, little girl...Remember what matters here. It's not about going back to the bad experience and finding something good about it. It's not finding good in the people involved. It's about you, today. What can YOU do with that, from where you are now?*

*Oh, okay, got it. I survived. I am resilient. I will create an environment where my kids feel safe to speak to me about anything when/if I become a mom. I will love my body and cherish it. I will not hurt it like Mr. Peter did. I will remember that my fear of powerful men is a reaction to my trauma. That fear is only trying to protect me from being violated again, but it has resulted in coping mechanisms that are not good for me in the long run. To start, I deserve partners that can pull their own weight. I understand that now and will try to seek men who are more my match. I also need to understand all the triggers that night created in me. I need to tell someone about this. Maybe I will look for a therapist or counselor to help me figure out how to do this? I...*

She did not know what else to add. It was a lot to think about, and she knew that healing would take much more than her writing a few words tonight. However, it was a start. She decided to move on to Demon #2.

## DEMON #1 — YOUR TURN NOW...

Do you see yourself in this chapter? What is your Demon #1? Has your innocence or childhood been violated? Are you okay with thinking about it? If so, write it down and proceed to the next question. If not, stop, breathe, and listen to your heart. Only do what it tells you to do. Write down how you feel right now. Do not rush your healing. Just breathe...

_____

_____

_____

_____

_____

_____

_____

_____

_____

_____

What fears, habits, or mindset did Demon #1 cause you to have? Are you okay with thinking about it? If so, write it down and proceed to the next question. If not, stop, breathe, and listen to your heart. Only do what it tells you to do. Write down how you feel right now. Do not rush your healing. Just breathe...

_____

_____

_____

_____

_____

_____

_____

_____

_____

What can you use or what have you used from that experience to better your life? If you can answer, please do so. If it gets to be too much, stop, breathe, and listen to your heart. Only do what it tells you to do. Do not rush your healing. Just breathe...

_____

_____

_____

_____

_____

_____

_____

_____

_____

_____

_____

# Demon #2 — The Betrayed Child

As hard as it was for her to think about Mr. Peter, the next incident that lodged yet another emotional wound into her heart also was horrible and she felt it had messed her up really badly for years, maybe for life. *Writing this part is not going to be easy,* she thought, *but it had to be done. Okay. Let's do this...*

Everybody makes mistakes. That is what they say, right? There is not one person she knew who had not used this phrase at least once. People fuck up. They err. They do stupid things. Usually, those sayings came out of the mouths of people who had fucked up themselves. As much as those phrases sometimes felt like a cop-out to her, she couldn't deny that she, too, had to use them a few times in her life. Like the time she gave the wrong address by mistake and the food delivery never made it to her get-together with her friends. That was just a mistake. However, in the case of her former friend Keera, what she did to her was not a mistake. It was intentional.

*Did Keera realize what she did to me that night?* The Keera incident was yet again one she tried her best to sweep under the rug in vain. For someone who did not trust too many people, she had been so open with Keera that it used to scare her sometimes. Keera knew everything. She knew too much. She was her unofficial therapist, her best friend, and her confidant, all at once. She had hidden the ugliness of her childhood from most people in her life, but when it came to Keera, she was powerless. One look from her caused all her hidden emotions to come out of her mouth with no control or restraint. "Come on, tell me what's wrong," Keera would plead with her. When those penetrating hazel eyes met hers, she always caved.

She did not like looking into Keera's eyes. And she knew that although it resulted in her spilling the beans more often than not, there was another reason why she kept her head down. Keera's eyes were more than a truth serum; they were the eyes of the girl she loved.

Before meeting Keera, she had never looked at girls as anything but friends and classmates. Some girls in middle school had quietly spoken about crushes on other girls, but it was never her thing. Never in a million years did she think she could ever be attracted to a girl, but that was before she met Keera and looked into her hazel eyes.

Those eyes were the sun, the moon, and the stars to her, for she had found in them the light and hope she longed for in everything else in her life. If Keera only knew how much she dreamed of kissing her sweet lips and holding her tight in the dark, she probably would have ended the friendship long ago. However, for years she kept her feelings a secret, as she was willing to sacrifice her heart rather than try pursing a relationship and risk losing Keera forever. But Keera did find out. After all, Keera's eyes were her truth serum, and on that one day she could not avoid them.

*Why did you have to look at me so intensely that night, Keera? Why?* She asked herself that question over and over again. That fateful day was the beginning of the end. It all started with a day at the beach and too much alcohol in the cooler. Later in the evening, she and Keera were the only ones left on the sand. As they talked about life and schools and hopes and dreams, she slipped: "I think you are so hot, I'd want to be with you if you were into girls." The moment she said it, she knew she had messed up.

"What did you just say?" asked Keera.

"I was just joking," she responded, attempting to save face and brush it off as a gaffe.

"I know you, don't lie to me. Please don't. Did you mean what you said? Come on, look at me. Look at me in the eye and tell me what you meant." How could she resist those eyes? She was doomed. She was caught. And so, she opened the floodgates of emotions she had been restraining for years and admitted to Keera that she was indeed in love with her. Keera listened, said she understood, said she wasn't into girls, but said that if they both wanted to be just friends, nothing would change. She also promised to take this admission to her grave and keep her secret safe, forever. Unfortunately, something did change, and something was revealed.

In fact, everything changed for good, and for the worse, a few weeks later at a party, where she accidently kissed Keera's boyfriend, Derek. He looked so much like her old boyfriend Kyle, and she had had way too much to drink that night. Indeed, she had been drinking heavily since she confessed her love for Keera at the beach.

Although Keera had assured her things were still the same between them, something had changed. They did not see each other much anymore, and she was heartbroken over losing not only her best friend, but also the love of her life. That night at the party, she poured herself drink after drink, and many shots of vodka later, she had forgotten where she was, what year it was, and who she was with. As she made her way to the kitchen, Derek came in to grab a beer and saw her barely standing up. He offered to help her find a seat. In her intoxicated, broken-hearted head, all she saw was Kyle coming back to her, and she leaned over to give him kiss. But it wasn't Kyle.

The moment Keera came in the kitchen with Derek behind her, she quickly sobered up and understood she was in trouble. The beautiful hazel eyes that usually looked at her with friendship and affection were now full of disdain. *Please Keera, my love, please do not look at me like that. I am sorry, I made a mistake. I was drunk. I am drunk.* As she waited for yelling or screaming or worse, silence, a crowd had gathered in the kitchen, most likely aware of the stupid thing she had just done.

After a few minutes of silence, Keera uttered the words that would cut her heart open and still haunt her years later: "Don't worry, Derek, she doesn't like you. She only pretends to like guys. She is a lesbian. She's mad because I rejected her months ago. Let's go. I cannot be friends with a messed-up girl like this anymore."

Years later, Keera still had those beautiful hazel eyes. Derek was no longer her boyfriend. He was now her husband. She knew this because she found their social media accounts and made it a point to keep track of their lives. It wasn't an obsession, but deep down she knew it was unhealthy. Yet the hurt caused by that evening had not left her heart. As much as she tried not to admit it, she was still reeling from what she had perceived as a betrayal from her best friend. Her occasional attraction to women was something she had not been comfortable with. She did not even know if she was bisexual or a lesbian at all. She just felt what she had felt but was not ready to put a label on it and announce it to the world — especially not the way Keera had done it.

The sound of the nurse coming to check on her briefly interrupted her thoughts on the Keera incident. After the nurse left, she realized that it wasn't one demon that was created from it, but two. One carried the pain of being betrayed by Keera breaking her promise and sharing her secret, and the other carried the guilt, shame, and self-loathing from betraying her best friend by kissing Derek. She knew that Demon #3 would have to address the emotional scars of what she had done to Keera by kissing Derek. Yes, Demon #3 was the one who carried shame and guilt for betraying a friend. In the meantime, though, she needed to continue writing about Demon #2 and what it did to her.

Since that party where she lost her best friend, Keera, she had closed off her heart to deep friendships and had become skeptical of anyone trying to get too close to her. Anyone wanting to get to know her in a deep way was a trigger for her. Every time someone started asking questions about her childhood or adolescence, she felt they were trying to get secrets from her that they would later blow out into the open in some kind of retaliation. She did not trust those who got too close.

If the pain of being betrayed was not hard enough, on top of that a shroud of shame started to engulf her sexuality. Although she had only dated men since, she had never stopped being attracted to some women. She just never pursued it, as it made her feel embarrassed and disgraceful.

One of her triggers was when people asked a question about her clothing style or her fashion sense. She was a tomboy. She wore pants and almost never wore a dress or a skirt. When someone asked her anything about her outfits, she would get triggered and become defensive because she felt as if they were suspecting her secret attraction to women. Suppressing that part of her sexuality and identity created angst, uneasiness, and fears that she had to numb with illegal substances and other unhealthy habits.

She now realized that Keera's betrayal had also caused her to put up walls around herself for her own protection. Unfortunately, those walls she put up were slowly becoming a fortress that trapped her. In keeping the world at bay, she had deprived herself of the joy of true friendships and close relationships. Something had to change before she cut herself away from the world for good. Maybe something could finally start changing tonight?

*Deep breaths, my girl…So, okay. How can I possibly make anything good out of this? Remember, it is not about turning what happened into a good thing. It is about what you can take from it from where you are now. Today.*

*Okay. For one, I need to be responsible with my drinking or stop altogether. I cannot get to the point where I am not able to control my actions due to being too drunk. I do see now how my drinking habit is just another coping mechanism to help me forget what I had been through. I did admit I was attracted to girls, and saying it to Keera did not kill me. So, I need to rethink why I am keeping it a secret, even today. Spying on Keera on social media is keeping me from releasing that pain in my life. It cannot* be good for my mental health. I may need to cut that out. Not everyone is Keera, and not everyone betrays. I have to try to remember that, too. My fear of getting close with people is there to prevent another Keera situation, but also it keeps me from having strong bonds with people. I have to find a way to forgive Keera, for my own sake and my own inner peace. I think I can deal with these demons by myself, at least for now. Okay… next demon.

## DEMON #2 — YOUR TURN NOW...

Do you see yourself in this chapter? What is your Demon #2? Do you carry the pain of being betrayed by someone you trusted and loved? Are you okay with thinking about it? If so, write it down and proceed to the next question. If not, stop, breathe, and listen to your heart. Only do what it tells you to do. Write down how you feel right now. Do not rush your healing. Just breathe…

_____

_____

_____

_____

_____

_____

_____

_____

_____

What fears, habits, mindset did Demon #2 cause you to have? Are you okay with thinking about it? If so, write it down and proceed to the next question. If not, stop, breathe, and listen to your heart. Only do what it tells you to do. Write down how you feel right now. Do not rush your healing. Just breathe...

_____

_____

_____

_____

_____

_____

_____

_____

_____

What can you use or what have you used from that experience to better your life? If you can answer, please do so. If it gets to be too much, stop, breathe, and listen to your heart. Only do what it tells you to do. Do not rush your healing. Just breathe...

_____

_____

_____

_____

_____

_____

_____

_____

_____

# Demon #3 — The Betrayer Child

"Guilt is perhaps the most painful companion of death." She had once read this quote attributed to Coco Chanel, and she fully understood what it meant. The emotional traumas inflicted on her by others were one thing, but the shame and guilt of what she did to others ate at her and made her feel disdain for the person she was.

The Keera incident, as she acknowledged moments prior while writing about Demon #2, also created Demon #3 — the self-loathing, self-hating demon that judged her and blamed her for a lot of the turmoil she had experienced in life.

For years and years, she had replayed the incident of that night at the party with Keera and Derek and wished she could go back and not kiss Derek. As much as she was disappointed in Keera for blurting out her secret to everyone at the party, she felt more disappointed in herself for the kiss, which she considered betraying her friend.

Yes, she did betray Keera, and that weighed on her a lot. How could she have been so reckless? Keera was everything to her. She was there for her through thick and thin, and this is how she repaid her? By kissing her boyfriend? She knew she was drunk but could not solely blame the alcohol. *I was a bad friend,* she thought. *I was not loyal and should have had the strength to stop myself from making such a mistake. Maybe I deserved to be betrayed in return by Keera for the hurt the kiss had caused her. Maybe I deserved the punishment?*

The demon forged out of the shame and guilt of that day had

affected her self-esteem in various negative ways. It contributed to her low self-esteem, as she thought she was a bad person. She blamed herself for things that were not her fault because she did not think she was a good person at her core. The shame and guilt of that day also affected the relationships and friendships she had since that fateful evening at the party with Keera. Every time she had a falling-out with a friend or a significant other, she told herself that she was the reason why things did not work out and convinced herself that she could not be a good friend to anyone. She also did not feel comfortable around other people's spouses, boyfriends, or girlfriends, for she had lost confidence in her ability to be a loyal friend and feared she would fall in love with her friends' significant others. *I can't go through that again,* she told herself. *I cannot risk betraying people I love again. I just can't do it.*

As a result of dealing with this demon and trying to prevent a similar situation from happening again, she put up walls and tried not to get close to anyone. Her lack of healthy self-esteem also led her to endure mistreatment from others, especially in romantic relationships, for she felt she needed to be punished for her betrayal that day. She did not know at the time why she accepted being treated poorly by many in her life, but sitting in her hospital bed, she realized that Demon #3 had greatly impacted her life in negative and destructive ways. Now what?

*Okay, what can I do with this demon?*

*To start, I have to find a way to release the shame and guilt I am carrying from betraying Keera. Maya Angelou said, "Do the best you can until you know better. Then when you know better, do better." I have to realize that I did not intentionally plan to betray my friend Keera at the party. Nevertheless, I have to take responsibility for what I did. And I did apologize to Keera about it when we were still on speaking terms. That awful night, I made a mistake; I must find a way to forgive myself, just like I have to find a way to forgive Keera. I cannot let this demon continue to make me feel like I am a bad person and an even worse friend. It is done, it's in the past, and I cannot make myself keep paying for it forever and rob myself of the joy of being close to others. Controlling my attachment to alcohol can also help with healing this pain since I can think clearer and make better choices when I am sober. I may need help with this demon, as my self-esteem is in shambles now. God, please help me find help for this.*

## DEMON #3 — YOUR TURN NOW...

Do you see yourself in this chapter? What is your Demon #3? What have you done in your life that you feel ashamed of? Where do you feel you have betrayed others? Are you okay with thinking about it? If so, write it down and proceed to the next question. If not, stop, breathe, and listen to your heart. Only do what it tells you to do. Write down how you feel right now. Do not rush your healing. Just breathe...

_____

_____

_____

_____

_____

_____

_____

_____

What fears, habits, mindset did Demon #3 cause you to have? Are you okay with thinking about it? If so, write it down and proceed to the next question. If not, stop, breathe, and listen to your heart. Only do what it tells you to do. Write down how you feel right now. Do not rush your healing. Just breathe...

_____
_____
_____
_____
_____
_____
_____
_____
_____
_____

What can you use or what have you used from that experience to better your life? If you can answer, please do so. If it gets to be too much, stop, breathe, and listen to your heart. Only do what it tells you to do. Do not rush your healing. Just breathe...

_____
_____
_____
_____
_____
_____
_____
_____
_____

# Demon #4 — The Abandoned/ Rejected Child

There are no instructions when it comes to being a good parent or caretaker. You learn on the go. Parents are humans too. A parent's main responsibility is to provide a roof over your head. A parent cannot be a child's friend. One cannot become a mature adult until one forgives one's parents…

All her life she heard these sayings over and over and over from her own folks, from teachers at school, in movies and sitcoms, and from pretty much anywhere there were adults talking. It was a constant barrage of messages aimed at brainwashing children into accepting mistreatment and neglect from their parents, while forgiving them for doing a bad job. At least that is how she felt. To her, all these phrases were just excuses parents and caretakers came up with to justify letting down children they are supposed to protect.

"Your feelings? What about them?" her Uncle Marc would ask. When she dared mention something about being sad and depressed, he would look at her with disappointing and disapproving eyes and shake his head in disdain, anger, and shame. "I work my ass off at the insurance office to send you to the best schools, buy you the best clothes, and give you the food you want, and you are depressed? Wow! Kids these days are so ungrateful," he would murmur under his moustache. "You've got all a girl can ever ask for and you are still complaining?" he would yell. "Well, let me tell you about how it was for me growing up with nothing and then you tell me why the hell you are depressed, my dear..."

By the time he started going down the memory lane of his poor childhood, his parents' economic struggles, and his lack of wealth growing up, he had lost her again. She had heard this speech so many times she could recite it herself from memory. *Blah, blah, blah. I know. Same old story. I am so sick of it. You don't get it, Uncle. You still don't get it after I explained it to you over and over, like a million times already. You just don't get it!*

No, he did not get it. Neither did her Aunt Jessie, the nurse. The two of them seemed so focused on "providing" for her that they totally missed the mess that her life had become. They totally did not notice her slow but steady emotional decline into a dark hole of depression, loneliness, and even suicidal thoughts. They did not notice how her friends had stopped coming to the house and that she had become more and more of a recluse, a shadow of the bubbly girl she had once been. They did not approve of her change in fashion but attributed it to "teenage" things. Her dark eyeliner, black nail polish, baggy clothes, red lipstick, dark clothing, and concerning steady weight gain were all part of a "phase" she was going through, they thought, just like they experienced when they were young. *Don't you see what is happening to me?*

They did not see it. She was invisible. One day in class, a teacher asked what superpower the students would pick if they had the choice of choosing one for themselves. *Invisibility, of course,* she said. *That way people can't see me, and I can go wherever I want, steal what I want, and do what I want.* However, at home, invisibility was not a superpower. It was a curse...

*They don't see me,* she used to think. *They do not see my soul, my pain, my fears, my hurts. All they focus on is doing "their job" as caretakers, which meant providing for me. Nowhere in their parenting philosophy was nurturing and protecting a child's heart. For some reason, they felt* that only adults experienced emotional distress, sadness, and anger. In their eyes, as long as a child had food, was getting an education, and had a roof over his or her head, the child had all he or she needed to be happy. Even as adults, it seemed like feelings and emotions were not something they gave too much thought to. They were almost robot-like when it came to work, and the only way they let out some steam was during one of their frequent fights, while they were yelling at her or at news anchor on the television, or when they let their hair down during those exotic vacations or overnight getaways on a rich friend's yacht. Their pursuit of happiness could be boiled down to the pursuit of pleasure and of some type of high, whether from booze, drugs, or food, as on Thanksgiving, where the goal of the day seemed to be to stuff themselves until they passed out.

*Did these people really want to raise me, or was there no one else to take me after my parents failed at the job?* She used to ask herself this question often; too often, actually. She felt like an afterthought most of the time, like a burden her Uncle Marc and Aunt Jessie felt stuck with and were forced to carry with them all their lives. She already felt her parents did not love her enough to fix their lives and be responsible caretakers; Aunt Jessie and Uncle Mark did not pass the caregiver test, either. Was it because she was not lovable? If her aunt only took the time to look into her eyes and see her soul's frequent cries for help, she would have seen the fear in her when Mr. Peter came over.

That morning, when they picked her up from the babysitter's house after Mr. Peter had been there the night before, Uncle Marc would have noticed that the innocence she once showed had left her once sparkly eyes, if he only paid attention to her. Aunt Jessie would have seen the marks left by the tears that dripped over her face all night. They would have felt the despair she experienced every time they would drop her off with Mr. Peter's niece again. But they did not see that, for they did not see her.

They did not want to see her. As long as someone was willing to take her, they gladly dropped her off, like she was a burden they

65

were always trying to get rid of. All they wanted to do was work and go on vacation.

There were a lot of vacations. However, only a few involved her. It felt as if each year, before summer ended, her aunt and uncle suddenly realized they had not taken her on any trips and squeezed in a so-called family vacation to feel better about basically abandoning her the rest of the year.

Sometimes, it felt as if she spent more time at one of her aunt's friends' houses or another uncle's house than at her own. Ever since she could remember she had often been brought to some cousin, somewhere, sometimes late at night, so that her folks could go away for "us time" or "work," as they said. Many of those drop-offs ended up being boring, strange, uncomfortable stays where the main concern of her caretakers was to make sure she ate and slept.

Caring about her emotions, about her feelings of abandonment, about her not being happy where she was dropped off was not even an afterthought for these people. She wondered sometimes if her aunt knew of the marijuana her friend smoked in front of her all the time. Did her Uncle Marc know that the husband of her Aunt Becky walked around the house wearing a really tiny Speedo — and that it made her uncomfortable? Did her Aunt Jessie know what Mr. Peter did to her? She wondered...

Forgive your parents, they said...only then will you become an adult. *Well, I will never be an adult then, because there is no way I can ever forgive the two people who had the responsibility to care for me and totally screwed it up. I cannot forgive my aunt and uncle, either. Do they know what they left me with? More fears and more demons, that's what!*

The demon forged out of the abandoned child in her had led her to feel unlovable and invisible most of the time. *If my parents could not love me, who could?* She felt like no one ever really cared about her feelings. In her mostly short relationships, abandonment was always a big issue. The demon of the abandoned child in her was triggered every time someone spent time away from her or did not include her in their activities. Whenever a boyfriend went out with his buddies, she felt it was because she was not important enough for him to want to stay home. If a lover did not call her or text her for over an hour, she thought he was going to disappear and never come back.

She became clingy. She was always anticipating that someone she cared for was going to disappear from her life and discard her like she was nothing. To prevent that, she broke off relationships as soon as she felt abandoned so that *she* would be the one ending them first, and not the one being left behind. She had lost a few good soulmates and friends because of that. *How the hell am I going to make something good come out of this?* she thought.

Then her mind snapped back to the present, in her hospital bed. The sun had started to rise, and she knew she had to hurry up and finish her list. She was only admitted for an overnight stay and was going to be discharged in a few hours.

The unfamiliar setting of her hospital room gave her the setting she needed for this new phase she was entering. She did not know how she would handle being back to her old apartment with the alcohol and drugs and pills that would be available to her. She wanted to finish the list and finish it while she still had the willpower to do so.

*Okay, what can I do with this demon?*

*Well, for one, if and when I become a mom, I will pay special attention to my child's emotions. I never really tried to understand how my parents grew up. I am not ever going to excuse what they did, but maybe they couldn't give me what they never got from their parents. I have not seen them for months. Maybe keeping my distance can be a good thing. They know I am there if they need me, right? Maybe I can have a talk with them and tell them how I felt growing up? I've got to think about that one. What if they are not ready for that? I need to pay attention to my abandonment triggers in my relationships. Maybe I can discuss it with my boyfriend up front so he knows what bothers me about this subject? I may need help with this abandonment stuff. Maybe I need to speak to someone. We'll see.*

With the day moving along, she knew the list had to move along, as well...

DEMON #4 — YOUR TURN NOW...

Do you see yourself in this chapter? What is your Demon #4? Your abandonment fears and triggers? Are you okay with thinking about it? If so, write it down and proceed to the next question. If not, stop, breathe, and listen to your heart. Only do what it tells you to do. Write down how you feel right now. Do not rush your healing. Just breathe...

_____

_____

_____

_____

_____

_____

_____

_____

What fears, habits, or mindset did Demon #4 cause you to have? Are you okay with thinking about it? If so, write it down and proceed to the next question. If not, stop, breathe, and listen to your heart. Only do what it tells you to do. Write down how you feel right now. Do not rush your healing. Just breathe...

_____

_____

_____

_____

_____

_____

_____

_____

_____

What can you use or what have you used from that experience to better your life? If you can answer, please do so. If it gets to be too much, stop, breathe, and listen to your heart. Only do what it tells you to do. Do not rush your healing. Just breathe...

_____

_____

_____

_____

_____

_____

_____

_____

_____

# Demon #5 — The Ugly Child

The lady at the beauty salon: "Who is this, your niece?"

Her aunt: "Yes, she is."

The lady at the beauty salon: "How old is she?"

Her aunt: "She is 13. She is one of the best students in her class."

The lady at the beauty salon: "Thank God she is smart, because she is not that pretty at all."

Her aunt: (silence)

Her: (silence and sadness)

She never forgot that conversation, and it haunted her all her life. A year after that horrible day, she had ballooned to her highest weight to date. Her Aunt Jessie and Uncle Marc had taken her to many health specialists to try to curb her weight gain. As much as they tried to restrict her access to food, she always found ways to get her favorite donut or her favorite bag of chips. Eating was comforting to her, and she desperately needed to feel comforted.

She never ran into that lady at the beauty salon again, but that did not mean that the negative comments about her looks stopped. Not at all. In fact, they were numerous, and while they were less direct than the salon incident, they hurt as much, nonetheless, because they came from those who claimed to love her. More specifically, they came from her paternal grandmother, Ellen.

Grandma Ellen was relentless with her sarcastic remarks. Nothing was ever good enough for her. When she saw her granddaughter, she always had something to say about her body or her looks.

"In my days, girls did not wear pants."

"In my days, girls were more feminine."

"In my days, girls were thinner."

It was nonstop, and no one in her family even lifted a finger to try to stop this constant assault on her self-esteem. She felt like her grandmother enjoyed putting her down and relished the feeling of breaking her spirit. It did not help that at school no boy ever asked her out. Most likely it was because she wasn't pretty, she thought... *Maybe Grandma was right; maybe the lady at the beauty salon was right; maybe I should lose weight and dress more girly. Maybe that will make Grandma Ellen like me?*

And so, somewhere in her heart, the pain of being seen as ugly lodged itself in a ventricle and created demons, skeletons, and fears that haunted her to this day. One of the main side effects of this trauma was one of the deadliest: bulimia.

It all started with a stupid, foul burger so many years ago. As her weight started becoming a serious threat to her health, she had tried to avoid the foods she loved the most, which were exactly the same foods that were forbidden by her doctor. Fast-food burgers were one of them. Something about the soft bun, the crunch of lettuce and tomato, the richness of mayo mixed with ketchup gave her the highest of the highs. It gave her a "food-gasm." There was not a week that went by without her indulging in her favorite burger at least three times.

Then one day, her favorite burger food truck was not at its usual location. She had gone through all social media to find out if it had just moved somewhere else, but there were no announcements. She grew desperate. *After what happened today, I need the burger fix,* she told herself. Indeed, that day had not been a good one.

A few hours before discovering the food truck was nowhere to be found, she was with a group of so-called friends celebrating the upcoming wedding of a girl she met a few years before. She did not particularly want to come, but the rejected child in her constantly needed to be accepted, and so she forced herself to participate in many things she did not want to. Feeling miserable and bored at events was a regular thing for her, and when she attended them, she often ended the night with her favorite vodka.

The celebratory brunch was going well until someone made a comment about her pants. It had taken her hours to get ready, for she had a hard time finding clothes that did not make her feel like a cow. Most of her closet was full of black clothes, for she felt they hid her ballooning weight the best. The pants in question were ones she saved for special occasions, as they made her look the best, she thought. When the person at the brunch pointed out a small hole in the seam of her pants, the ugly child in her woke up, triggered. That ugly child was triggered every time anyone commented on weight, even if the conversation was not about her. She hated fashion shows and social media stars who constantly posted pictures of themselves at unrealistic weights that were unachievable without huge financial investments in personal trainers and plastic surgeons. Although she bit her tongue and managed to stay relatively calm throughout the rest of the bridal brunch, tension was building up inside her and she needed her burger fix.

The food truck was not there. It was nowhere. Desperate for the food fix, she drove until she found a questionable pizza and burger joint, then went in to place an order. The three burgers she purchased did not make it the whole way back home, as she ferociously gobbled up every single one of them. A few hours later she started feeling bloated and nauseated, and thought about the bad feelings she had walking into the dingy pizza joint earlier. Something had told her that the place was not too sanitary, but she overlooked her intuition to satisfy her cravings. *I'm going to pay for this*, she thought, thinking that an upset stomach or food poisoning were the worst things that could come from eating these terrible burgers. They weren't. These burgers were going to end up sending her down a toxic rabbit hole that would take her years to crawl out of.

A few hours after she binged on the burgers, she knew something was not right. An intense feeling of nausea had her running to the bathroom every five minutes. However, nothing was coming out. Finally, at the end of her wits, she put her finger down her throat to try to help the purge. Boy did the bad stuff come out then — buns, meat, lettuce, everything. After a few minutes, she started feeling relief and found the strength to get on her feet and wash up. As she rinsed her mouth, she couldn't help but notice her stomach was flat. She felt empty inside and the feeling was intoxicatingly good. It was like a high. *Hmmm*, she thought. *I can eat and throw the food out and the calories too? And the fat? And everything?*

Another thing that felt good was that she was not hungry. You would think that after emptying her stomach she would have felt hungry, right? No. The slight presence of nausea and the exhaustion of throwing up took way her appetite. All of a sudden, the ugly and fat child in her felt she could finally do things to suppress her constant hunger. *Yes*, she thought. *I can have my cake and eat it too.* Well, in her case, she could have her cake, enjoy it, throw it up, and not suffer the consequences of the extra calories.

She was in control now, she felt. She could eat all she wanted and then get rid of it. What she didn't know was that the so-called benefits of this habit would eventually cost her dearly. It did work for a few years, and she lost a considerable amount of weight. However, over time, it stopped dropping and her bulimia only helped her maintain a level that she was not too happy with. In addition to that disappointment, her bulimia would also cause her to throw up in unsanitary public bathrooms, cause her to freak out when she did not make it to the bathroom on time and the food had already digested, cause her to damage her digestive system, and cause her to lie time and time again when she had to excuse herself to throw up unnoticed.

*Now, in the hospital after her car accident, she carefully considered what could be good about this demon. This demon makes me hate my body and engage in unhealthy habits to try to make it "pretty." How can I find anything positive in that? Okay, think, girl, think! Well, having gone through this, maybe I can relate to other girls with body image issues? The demon of the ugly child got me involved in toxic eating habits so that I can feel pretty and not feel bad about my looks. Maybe when I become a mom, I will always give positive feedback to my kids on how they look. Maybe I learned that binging and then purging only brings temporary comfort but long-term damage. I throw up to feel better about my body after I binge eat to feel better about my emotional scars. It is a toxic cycle, and I don't know how to stop it. Maybe I need professional help with this one. Well, that's all I got for now. Time is going and they will discharge me soon. I better move on to Demon #6.*

## DEMON #5 — YOUR TURN NOW…

Do you see yourself in this chapter? What is your Demon #5? Your self-image demon? Are you okay with thinking about it? If so, write it down and proceed to the next question. If not, stop, breathe, and listen to your heart. Only do what it tells you to do. Write down how you feel right now. Do not rush your healing. Just breathe…

_____

_____

_____

_____

_____

_____

_____

_____

_____

What fears, habits, mindset did Demon #5 cause you to have? Are you okay with thinking about it? If so, write it down and proceed to the next question. If not, stop, breathe, and listen to your heart. Only do what it tells you to do. Write down how you feel right now. Do not rush your healing. Just breathe…

_____
_____
_____
_____
_____
_____
_____
_____
_____

What can you use or what have you used from that experience to better your life? If you can answer, please do so. If it gets to be too much, stop, breathe, and listen to your heart. Only do what it tells you to do. Do not rush your healing. Just breathe…

_____
_____
_____
_____
_____
_____
_____
_____
_____

# Demon #6 — The Unprotected Child

As she looked at the clock in her hospital room, she knew she was not going to have time to list all her demons. She would just have time for Demon #6, and maybe one more, and would have to wrap this up soon. Then, as she wrote the name of the sixth demon, she knew it would be her most painful passage thus far.

In every room of her home there was an image or statue of the Archangel Saint Michael and Our Lady of Fatima. A picture of Saint Michael also was in her car, her purse, basically everywhere. Having been raised Catholic, she had learned about this archangel being the head of the celestial army, the one who protected the Kingdom of God. He was the saint people prayed to when they were being mistreated my others, the saint who provided protection against heartbreak, betrayal, bad influences, and so on. She did not go anywhere without having something of Saint Michael on her person.

Her fears were so strong that she felt she needed constant protection. She could not understand, in her fragile emotional state, that needing protection all the time meant she was telling the universe that she felt unsafe all the time. Those thoughts of not being safe were only attracting threatening people and situations to her life. The Law of Attraction states that we attract what we constantly think about. She had heard that once in a motivational seminar she attended but she did not realize that it also applied to bad things too. She did not understand that what she focused on all the time was what she was calling into her life. At the rate she was going with the need for protection, she was probably heading for a life of extreme paranoia and maybe worse.

*How did this all start?* she thought. *How did I start feeling unsafe all the time?* Well, for one, the Mr. Peter episode left her feeling unprotected and vulnerable. Her parents, who were supposed to watch out for her well-being, had casually left her defenseless — at the mercy of a wolf in sheep's clothing. When her aunt did not defend her against negative comments about her figure and looks at the beauty salon, she felt unprotected. When her Uncle Marc conveniently had to go out when Mr. Peter was alone in the house with her, she felt unprotected. All these situations led her to live in extreme fear, always anticipating harm to come her way. *What a sad way to live, little girl…*

Having Saint Michael items all over her home, office, and car was still not enough to make her feel totally safe. She did not trust people with her personal information and rarely signed up for anything online. She put several cameras around her home to protect herself from would-be intruders. When it came to dating, she rarely used her real name and got annoyed whenever a date figured out certain truths about her. People asking questions about her life was a huge trigger. When someone requested her email address at a chain pharmacy, she got offended and argued with the cashier about why the information was needed for her to buy her items. When mail would come to her that she did not expect, she wondered if she was a victim of identity theft.

When she could not find her debit card, she called her bank and canceled it right away, only to find it five minutes later 95 percent of the time. She was always afraid to ride in a car with only one person, and she preferred taking the bus rather than getting a ride home. That is why when an emotional wellness coach asked her, a few years ago, if she was fear-based, the only answer that fit her was yes.

*Feeling unprotected has really hindered my life,* she thought. Although she had become aware of some of her fears, it wasn't until she thought about it and put her feelings down on paper that she realized the severity of the impact that feeling unsafe had on her life.

Now what? How could she come up with any positive about this problem and those demons that fear had created in her?

She thought about that. *Well, for one, the fear of people getting my personal details has made me less vulnerable to online hacking and identity theft, since I do not do any business online. At the same time, it has made me miss out on some deals, some connections, and other valuable things. Maybe I can research a secure way to at least start being part of the online world.*

When she was younger, as she wrote into her diary, she sometimes thought about publishing some of her writings. *Well, if I can muster the courage to tap into online resources, maybe I can give myself the opportunity to showcase my writing skills and stop repressing my talents,* she thought. Repressing her passion for writing had cost her more than she could imagine.

Maya Angelou famously wrote that "there is no greater agony than bearing an untold story inside you." She was right. Fearing the loss of privacy along with the exposure of her addictions, bad experiences, and bad actions had been the main reasons why she did not write, and it was slowly destroying her on the inside. Someone had told her that a lot of the angst people carry with them is related to the fact that they are not living the life their spirits want them to enjoy. A lot of the stress we have is from not giving ourselves room *to be ourselves* and not using our individual talents to enrich the world and showcase that part of the universal light that lives within us.

Suppressing her gifts was indeed causing her stress and agony. It had to stop. She did not know how she would deal with this demon, but she knew she had to find a way to better manage her fears.

With little time left before she would be discharged, she knew she would not have time to list all her demons and reflect on them. She had exposed some of the big ones so far and knew there was one more she had to write about. She decided to take time the following weeks to think about the other demons and their triggers and fears, but she was confident that the major ones had been addressed.

Well, there *was* still one more big one: The Healed Adult.

## DEMON #6 — YOUR TURN NOW . . .

Do you see yourself in this chapter? What is your Demon #6? The side of yourself that feels unsupported and unprotected? Are you okay with thinking about it? If so, write it down and proceed to the next question. If not, stop, breathe, and listen to your heart. Only do what it tells you to do. Write down how you feel right now. Do not rush your healing. Just breathe...

_____

_____

_____

_____

_____

_____

_____

_____

What fears, habits, mindset did Demon #6 cause you to have? Are you okay with thinking about it? If so, write it down and proceed to the next question. If not, stop, breathe, and listen to your heart. Only do what it tells you to do. Write down how you feel right now. Do not rush your healing. Just breathe...

_____

_____

_____
_____
_____
_____
_____
_____
_____
_____

What can you use or what have you used from that experience to better your life? If you can answer, please do so. If it gets to be too much, stop, breathe, and listen to your heart. Only do what it tells you to do. Do not rush your healing. Just breathe...

_____
_____
_____
_____
_____
_____
_____
_____
_____
_____

# Demon #7 — The Healed Adult

*No more boogeyman to blame. It's all on you, dear.*
*It's your problem now.*

She was very much an analytical person. Everything she experienced had to be examined, questioned, criticized, reexamined in that head of hers. She liked being able to understand how things happened from start to finish. One of the main ways she loved to look at situations was from the perspective of cause and effect. At the core of this life philosophy of hers was a strong sense of justice and accountability. Indeed, it was important to her that credit is given to those who performed good deeds, while blame is laid squarely at the feet of those responsible for bad actions. What she did not realize until later was that things were not always that simple.

Her penchant toward this sort of accountability was partially rooted in the fact that she felt she did not get justice for a lot of the horrible things she went through in her life. They say sometimes that people seek to give what no one gave to them. One of her coworkers had made this observation during one of the volunteer events they had attended together. "You see," her colleague said, "a lot of these people come and help all the time. They almost become obsessed with serving others. Sometimes, I think they give so much because they have a void inside — a hole that they are trying to fill by giving others what was never given to them." She had heard her coworker's words but still wrestled with the concept years later, as she believed that some people wanted to do good just to do good, and not for some unconscious self-serving urge to heal a hidden childhood wound.

Whatever her motives were, she always felt strongly about justice and accountability, especially when it came to what others did. And she felt this way again a few hours earlier when she realized her demons had gotten her to crash into the lake. Accountability here was a no-brainer, she thought. *It is clear that my emotional wounds, which don't heal and keep hurting, are what drove me to lose my temper, storm out of the party, and drive absentmindedly. And the people who created those demons are to blame for what has been happening to me. Yes, my life is fucked up because of Mr. Peter and my teacher and my parents and Keera and the bullies in my freshman year and the crappy neighborhood I grew up in — they are all responsible for my demise, for almost getting me killed tonight. If I misbehave or if I end up screwing up my life, it is because of them. All of them. It is their fault. I have people to blame. It is not my fault.*

*But it is your car now, my girl…*

A few weeks ago, she had started hearing some knocking around the rear tires of her car. She was pretty good at maintaining her vehicle and bringing it in for regular oil changes and wheel alignment. When the knocking wouldn't stop, she had finally decided to bring the car to her mechanic, Michael.

Michael was the closest thing to a wise older brother she could ever have. However, she dreaded going to him because he reminded her of her old friend Keera. He had those piercing eyes that seemed like they could see through all of her bullshit and acting. He had a habit of saying the right thing that brought tears to her eyes and made her remember a wound, but he did not do it forcefully or directly. As he commented on a car issue, he would always turn their conversation into a wisdom lesson and use the car problem as a metaphor for a real-life issue.

When she bought the car to Michael that day, he quickly figured out that one of her rear axles needed to be replaced. That was not what she wanted to hear. She had just bought the car and was promised all worked well. "I got sold a lemon!" she complained.

"No," said Michael. "You bought an old car with problems that may have started with the previous owner, but it is your car now. It is your problem now. No matter who did what before, it is now your responsibility to either fix it or get another one, but you can't go back and blame the past. You have the keys. It is your car now, and you have to take the responsibility to get it back on track or get rid of it."

Once again, Michael left her perplexed, wondering if he was taking about the car or her life. What was his point? *Now that the car is mine, I can't keep looking for people to blame and I have to take responsibility for it myself? Even if the problem is not my fault?*

*The answer is yes, child. And Michael was, indeed, taking about your life. You know it.*

The answer was yes about the car, and the answer was yes about her life. For years she relied on excuses to justify her unproductive and negative actions and reactions. Everything bad thing she said or did, she blamed on triggers, fears, demons, and skeletons. It was easy for her to use that reasoning to justify her behavior. The reasons *were her story*, like Tony Robbins had said at one of his motivational seminars. *We all have a story, or stories. I am like this because…I am like that because…*But we forget that at one point we all become adults and we get the keys to the car or to the house. And at that point, it becomes our problem. No boogeyman to blame, no fault to assign. No. Just the realization that it is on us to fix us. And that realization is not easy.

*The Healed Adult is a demon?* she thought. Yes, it was. It is. And it, too, is rooted in fear. Fear of being responsible for *all* of her actions, reactions, and behaviors. Indeed, the Healed Adult was the wounded child who would have to take all the blame for her anger, explosion, bulimia, cutting, addictions, and other issues. It would be the child who would have to fix what others broke. And that wasn't fair, she felt. *Why do I have to fix something I didn't break? Isn't that giving a pass to those who hurt me? That is not fair!*

*But it is your car now, my girl…*

*It is your car, your heart, your soul, your body. It is yours. Therefore, it is your responsibility, my love. Life is not about fairness sometimes. It is about making a decision to live. Fully. Happily. Peacefully. It is about forgiving others, not for their sakes, but for your own inner peace. It is about seeking legal or moral justice when you can do so safely, but also letting go when you can't. It is about fixing the house after you bought it because it is yours now. It is your life, my child. Take ownership and run it your way. With responsibility also comes control and dependence on yourself and not others. Take control of your life now, my child!*

*If I am no longer a victim, who am I?*

Who are you? Who are you, little girl? Who are you without your story? Without your emotional wounds? Who will you be once you heal your pain? *Wait a minute… a life with no pain? That couldn't be not possible. No way.*

Pain was her destiny. Her karma. Her luck. Her deal. Her thing. Her identity. What do you mean, a life without pain?

*I am the girl who went through a lot,* she would think. Although she had hardly mentioned anything about the horrors she had lived through, she occasionally let slip to her friends that she had been through a lot in her life. Some who knew her felt that instinctively, without her saying a thing — the liquor store owner who saw her in his store frequently, the coworkers who smelled alcohol on her breath early in the morning, the friends who witnessed her constant outbursts every time something triggered her, the gym coach who used to see her spend way too long punching those bags in the back. They all knew it, and in their own way, they all tried to help her, even if the help was a crutch she had leaned on for too long.

*Who are you without your pain, little girl?*

*You are a child of God. You are a star in the galaxy. You are an intentional creation of the universe. You are not meant for a life of endless suffering. Remember that your light may get dimmed but can never be extinguished while you are alive, as Maya Angelou explained. Rise and* become who you were always meant to be: a little piece of the sun. Pain is a part of life and will come to you here and there. However, in between painful experiences, you can heal your wounds with time and experience moments, days and years of joy and peace, little girl. You can! You can start anew the moment you decide to and reclaim your life.

She would one day not only believe that, but know that, with conviction. It would take a little while, though.

I do not want to get used to being a victim forever! I refuse. I'm tired of all this chaos and demons and fears and drinking and throwing up and crashing and everything! I'm tired of it all! In that instant, her heart smiled because it knew its little girl was finally on her way back...

Although it would take her years to fully understand the power of these words and to fully live by them, in that moment, in the hospital, everything had changed. Author Paulo Coelho says that once we want something, the entire universe conspires to help us in achieving it. Well, he must have been right, for once she said no to victimhood and meant it, she felt a strength, a courage, a fire she had never felt before. For once in her life, she felt the universe was with her, behind her, and that it would help her heal. She thought of her maternal grandmother, who she missed every day since she had passed away when she was a teenager. She felt her grandma cheering her on.

"You walk to that demon closet and heal your old wounds, okay? I will be here to watch over your heart and hold the fort down while you take care of yourself. Go ahead. I got you."

As she closed her eyes, she could hear her grandma telling her this and knew it wasn't a dream. She had been alone in so many fights in her life, but in this one, she wasn't going to be. Little did she know that the love and support she felt from the afterlife and from within herself would be equally matched in the months and years to come by the number of people, many influential, who would suddenly start making their way into her life to help her achieve even bigger healing goals than what she had ever dreamed of. Little did she know, she would one day not only heal her pain, but use her wisdom from her own healing to help the entire world heal.

"I am ready," she said out loud. "I am ready to face demons and hopefully find a way to heal them, eventually."

And so, she looked down and saw that she only had one piece of paper left. She had to make this last page count. *What will I use this for?* she asked herself. *I've listed all of my main demons; I've tried to look at them with a different perspective. I now understand that my triggers, my bulimia, my demons, and my fears were coping mechanisms I have been using because I still carry the pain of old heartaches. My demons are causing a lot of negativity in my life, but they are part of me, and I need to work with them — to understand them and to release their pain, so I can release mine. I don't know how I will go about healing, but writing this down today feels like a start.*

*I guess there is only one thing left for me to do before I get discharged. I need to let my demons know that I have acknowledged them and that I know why they are in pain too. I have to tell them I will take the wheel of my life now. I must thank them for trying to keep me safe from the pain of remembering old wounds, and pushing me to indulge in activities and behaviors that provided relief from my inner turmoil, although the relief always was short-lived. Not facing past hurts, pushing them under the rug, only led me to slow self-destruction on the inside. I have to ask my demons to forgive me for hating them as my enemies for all those years rather than trying to heal them..*

She lifted her pen one last time and wrote the following words: "Okay, Demons, we need to talk…"

## DEMON #7 — YOUR TURN NOW …

Do you see yourself in this chapter? How has your Demon #7 manifested in your life? The side of yourself that feels afraid to be responsible for your good and your bad actions?

Are you okay with thinking about it? If so, write it down and proceed to the next question. If not, stop, breathe, and listen to your heart. Only do what it tells you to do. Write down how you feel right now. Do not rush your healing. Just breathe...

_____

_____

_____

_____

_____

_____

_____

_____

_____

What fears, habits, mindset did Demon #7 cause you to have? Are you okay with thinking about it? If so, write it down and proceed to the next question. If not, stop, breathe, and listen to your heart. Only do what it tells you to do. Write down how you feel right now. Do not rush your healing. Just breathe...

_____

_____

_____

_____

_____

_____

_____

_____

_____

What can you use or what have you used from that experience to better your life? If you can answer, please do so. If it gets to be too much, stop, breathe, and listen to your heart. Only do what it tells you to do. Do not rush your healing. Just breathe…

_____

_____

_____

_____

_____

_____

_____

_____

_____

_____

# An Apology to My Demons

*Dear Demons:*

*I have hated you my whole life. You have caused me so much grief, aggravation, and fear that I cannot see how I will ever get to a point where I can stand you, let alone like you. However, yesterday I heard something that made me question the way I looked at you all. After reflecting on it a bit, I am starting to realize that you were born to protect me from going through pain again. I now understand that you all have gotten to the point where you are so wounded that you are lashing out, just like I am lashing out. The urgency of the situation calls for me to undergo a radical change of mindset, for I know today that I no longer have the luxury of inaction. I must make peace with you all before we destroy each other.*

*Now that I think about it, I actually do have a choice. I could choose to stay the course and let you demons send me to straight to the bottom of the lake, or I can fight to take back the wheel of my life and maybe have a shot at a decent future. After much reflection last night and this morning, and after yet another close call with death a few hours ago, I've decided to choose my heart and give myself a chance to heal. I chose to side with my heart today because it is the only thing that chooses me, every day, over and over, no matter what others do to it, and no matter what I, myself, put it though.*

*Until last night, I thought you demons were foreign enemies who infiltrated my being with the mission of destroying me from within. The toxic coping mechanisms, the bad habits, and the unjustified fears had brought me to many situations and people that were not good for me or good to me.*

*Now I see that you demons were just trying your best to stop me from getting into situations that would open old emotional wounds or remind me of them. I know that now. I understand what you were trying to do. As hard as it is for me to say this, thank you for trying to protect me. Thank you for trying to stop me from dealing with my emotional scars because you thought that would bring me sadness and grief. Thank you for making me crave food and substances that made me feel good so that I could forget the memories that still traumatize me to this day. I am sorry for thinking you were the bad guys. For that, I apologize.*

*However, as noble as your intentions were in trying to protect me, the unplanned consequences of you shielding me is that I never tried to deal with my past hurts. I never tried to heal them. I only did things to make me forget them, like using drugs and alcohol, or I tried to keep myself so busy that I would not have time to think about old pains too much. I just kept sweeping my emotions under the rug and never dealt with them. You demons know what happens when you don't take care of a problem. It festers and festers until it forces you to deal with it, or it causes some type of chaos and turmoil in your life. That is how I ended up in the lake last night.*

*Although I appreciate the reason for your existence and can now see that your goals were to keep me safe, please understand that having you guys run my life made me act and react from a place of fear and pain, rather than from a place of joy and self-love. As a result, I kept making bad choices. Looking at life through fear and pain cannot take me anywhere good and solid in the long run. Even though your influence was born out of love and provided me with short-term pleasure or distractions, it shielded me from taking responsibility for my actions. Because of that, I never felt accountability for reacting poorly when I* was triggered, and I shifted the blame of my poor behaviors to you, to my past, and to those who hurt me.

Make no mistake. Choosing to heal you, my demons, does not mean I excuse those who were responsible for some of those scars left on my heart. I have a lot to think about in terms of seeking justice for some of the wrongs that were done to me. I have to make sure I act safely if I confront certain people, so I will seek help to make the right decision about how to move forward. I know that more likely than not I will not get justice or closure from everyone who hurt me, and maybe from no one, so I know I may have to forgive people who are not repentant or sorry. It is okay, it will be okay, because I will forgive and let go for my own sake and not for theirs. I will cut the chains they put on my heart and not give them any power over my life anymore. At the end of the day, I need to forgive others, because ultimately, I need to also forgive myself for my own mistakes and poor judgment.

I know I may need help to go through this journey back to healing, to peace and inner joy, and I know there are people and places I can go to for assistance if I cannot do certain things alone. That is okay. It doesn't mean I am weak. In fact, it takes strength to ask for what I need, so I will ask for help if I need it.

My demons, you are part of me, as are my self-loving impulses. I cannot reject you or like only certain parts of myself. If I want to heal completely, I have to learn to integrate you all with my other sides and love the whole of me, you included.

Now what? Time to put all those survivor skills to use again, but differently this time. Yes. It probably will be a battle with you demons. You've existed since I got hurt, and you have your role and your purpose. You may feel threatened by this radical change of mindset I will be striving for...Trust me, no need to worry.

Let's talk, okay? Let's start healing. No need to be afraid that I will eliminate you all. I will not. That is not my end goal. If I destroy you, I will destroy myself, for you are part of my history and part of who I am today.

*You know what I really wish for, deep down? That all of you demons, and every other part of me, can one day all dance together and laugh together one day...Wouldn't that be beautiful? That is my wish, my demons. That is my wish...*

*Love,*
*Me*

# Epilogue

It would be years before she could dance with her demons, but as time went by, she slowly began healing and integrating them into her life. She worked on understanding the extent of her demons' effects on her mindset, life view, behavior, and actions. Nothing had been the same since the accident at the lake. The road to emotional healing was tough, and she had gone backward a few times. However, she never gave up and kept fighting for her heart.

She is still fighting today, for some wounds never fully heal. Every day she has to make the decision to be positive and hopeful, and she is not always successful at achieving that. However, her efforts are now easier and more routine. Everyone she meets can see light in her eyes and the sun in her smile. Surprisingly, she even got to a point where she could talk about some of her hardships without crying. That's how she knew she was healing.

She has not been hard on herself by setting some kind of deadline for when she would be fully healed emotionally. She takes her life one day at a time and pays attention to her actions, feelings, and reactions.

Self-reflection is something she does regularly, and that helps her catch herself right away when she is slipping into old habits and mind-sets. As Oprah Winfrey once said, "You cannot have a meaningful life without self-reflection." She believes in that sentiment and can see the benefits of taking time out to think about how her life was going.

When she reverts to negativity, she tries to forgive herself quickly and has mechanisms in place to ensure the negative mindset does not reoccur too frequently.

She is a work in progress, and that is perfectly okay with her.

As for her "pretend" acting career, it is pretty much over. No more Oscars.

Once in a while old fears cause her to say or do something out of fear of rejection, but for the majority of the time she is herself. Her appearance, her apartment, and her activities all reflect the real her she had hid for years. She even colored her hair blue, something she had been wanting to do for a while but was afraid would displease some of her friends and connections.

Not everyone celebrated the changes in her life. She lost some friends during the process and stopped going to some of the places she once loved. However, she is good with that. The few friends she has now are a fraction of the number of people she used to hang out with, but they are real friends who accept her for who she is.

One spring afternoon, she was sitting under a cherry blossom tree thinking about her life. Since her accident, she had spent more time in nature, as she felt it helped her heal and feel joy. She was now an avid hiker and had started an indoor and outdoor garden that she used for her nutrition. Sweet basil, Italian parsley, and thyme gave her kitchen a sweet and delicious smell. She was now cooking often, as she understood that real, true transformation had to be holistic. For real sustainable change to take root, one must get healthy at all levels at the same time: mind, body, spirit. She made time for herself and could see her inner light shining more and more every day...

As petals from the cherry blossom tree fell on her lap, she smiled and felt grateful for being able to enjoy its beauty. Being around cherry blossoms and oak trees always made her heart smile. Gratitude was now something she felt every day. It was her soul's song. It was her main spiritual practice. As she got up, the book she was reading fell. It was *I Know Why the Caged Bird Sings*, by Maya Angelou. She had read it multiple times, but only fully understood it after her lake accident, for she at one point was a caged bird too, who just wanted to be free. She felt an enormous feeling of gratitude as she grabbed the book, for it had been instrumental in her healing and transformation. As she walked toward her car, she remembered a Maya Angelou quote that had been on her mind for weeks: "When you learn, teach. When you get, give."

*Is that a sign?* she thought. Since her last brush with death, she had become very spiritual and was now fully open to receiving subtle messages from the universe.

*Maybe it is a sign*, she thought. *A sign that I should pay it forward, I think. Should I share what I know and hope it makes the road for someone else, just like Maya Angelou and countless others did for me?* She knew the answer to that. She had known the answer for years now.

And so, she took her turquoise diary, which she now carried with her everywhere she went, and she wrote yet another set of words that would change her life forever. It was a book title: *An Apology to My Demons.*

And one more title, and another title...*Get to work, little girl... You have so much more wisdom to share.* Nelson Mandela said, "As we let our own light shine, we unconsciously give other people permission to do the same."

Putting herself out there and telling the story of her struggles was a daunting task that scared her a bit. Once again, she was going to have to be strong and summon all the courage she possessed to speak her truth and not let the music die inside her, as they say. She was going to share what she learned from her suffering and healing, for she knew that somewhere out there was a broken little girl waiting to be inspired by her story — just as she had been by Maya Angelou and countless others.

## FINAL REFLECTIONS (FOR NOW)...

Does the Epilogue speak to you? How? What is the wisdom/talent you have that can make a difference in people's lives?

_____

_____

_____

_____

_____

_____

_____

_____

After reading this last section, do you feel ready to open your own demon closet? Do you see how your demons could have been created to protect your heart from getting hurt again? Are you okay with thinking about it? If so, proceed to the next question. If not, stop, breathe, and listen to your heart. Only do what it tells you to do. Write down how you feel right now. Do not rush your healing. Just breathe...

_____

_____

_____

_____

_____

_____

_____

_____